News Making
in the
Trial Courts

LONGMAN PROFESSIONAL STUDIES
IN POLITICAL COMMUNICATION
AND POLICY

Editorial Advisor: Jarol B. Manheim

Robert E. Drechsel   *News Making in the Trial Courts*

Forthcoming:

Roger W. Cobb and Charles D. Elder   *The Political Uses of Symbols*

Doris A. Graber   *Processing the News: How People Tame the Information Tide*

Myles Martel   *Debates in American Political Campaigns*

Brian Weinstein   *The Civic Tongue: Political Consequences of Language Choices*

News Making
in the
Trial Courts

Robert E. Drechsel
Colorado State University

Longman

New York & London

NEWS MAKING IN THE TRIAL COURTS

Robert E. Drechsel

Longman Inc., 1560 Broadway, New York, NY 10036
Associated companies, branches, and representatives
throughout the world.

Copyright © 1983 by Longman Inc.

Developmental Editor: Irving E. Rockwood
Editorial and Design Supervisor: Frances Althaus
Manufacturing and Production Supervisor: Anne Musso

Library of Congress Cataloging in Publication Data

Drechsel, Robert E. (Robert Edward)
  News making in the trial courts.

  (Longman professional studies in political communication
and policy)
  Bibliography: p.
  Includes index.
  1. Newspaper court reporting—United States. 2. Newspaper
court reporting—Minnesota. 3. Courts of first
instance—Minnesota. I. Title. II. Series.
PN4745.D7   070.4′49347731   81-17202
ISBN 0-582-28319-1   AACR2
ISBN 0-582-28318-3 (pbk.)

Manufactured in the United States of America

For My Mother and Father

Contents

Tables and Figures

Figure

Foreword

In this book Robert Drechsel helps draw together two seemingly dispa-
rate literatures, one focusing on the relationship between public officials
and reporters, the other on the behavior of judges and other actors in
courts of original jurisdiction. Readers familiar with the former will find
this work very much in the tradition of Nimmo, Dunn, Sigal and others
who have examined the interplay of motives and resources among those
who would (and do) make the news and those who are charged with con-
veying it to the public. Those familiar with the latter will find here a concern with the operation of the lower level judicial process consistent with
that presented in such recent works as those of Jacob, Eisenstein and
Alpert. Drechsel's blend of the two themes is unique and gives added
dimension to each.

The book reports the results of a study of the interaction of court personnel and attorneys with reporters covering the Minnesota state courts.
Based on a combination of survey research, extended interviews and participant observation, it offers insights into how news of the courts is
made, what exchanges take place among the parties to the process, and
how the product of these exchanges, which is to say the news, is viewed
by those most directly involved. The reader will come away from this
book with a better understanding of the workings of two institutions with
which Americans come into contact every day, the lower courts and the
media, and of the perceptions that each as an institution has of the other.
Such an understanding helps to put in context both the news of the courts
we do see and that we do not.

The monographs in this series are intended to illuminate the institutional and theoretical foundations of the communication process as political phenomena. Professor Drechsel's thoughtful analysis of news making
in the trial courts clearly fulfills this dual purpose.

Jarol B. Manheim
Blacksburg, Virginia

Acknowledgments

There seems to be no unique way to acknowledge the help and support of the many people behind a project like the study that follows. That is unfortunate, because I want them to know that my gratitude is sincere.

I shall begin with the Kaltenborn Foundation, whose financial assistance provided the resources that allowed me to do the research in more depth and breadth than I might otherwise have hoped. I owe much, too, to Cindy Cooper, former information officer for the Minnesota Supreme Court, whose interest in the project encouraged me and whose contacts with others in the legal-judicial community undoubtedly smoothed the way for their cooperation. Paul Westphal, director of the Minnesota Supreme Court's Office of Continuing Education for State Court Personnel, helped more than I can express. He provided valuable advice on the language of the survey questionnaires for judges and clerks and wrote cover letters urging judges and clerks to cooperate. Stephen Askew, executive director of the County Attorneys Council, helped by providing a cover letter encouraging county attorneys to cooperate, by providing the follow-up to increase survey response and by providing mailing lists. Frank Harris, director of the Minnesota Bar Association's Continuing Legal Education, supported the project, and he and his organization administered questionnaires to private attorneys at workshops in Minnesota.

I am also indebted to the attorneys, judges, court clerks and newspaper reporters who provided invaluable advice when the survey questionnaires were pretested. And, of course, I am grateful to the reporter, newspaper and sources who allowed me the access I needed for the observational portion of my research. Unfortunately, they must remain anonymous. Also deserving thanks is Roger Leduc, an excellent, now-graduated journalism student and friend at Colorado State University who did yeoman work by computerizing my raw data, by writing the necessary program for computer analysis and by troubleshooting when problems arose.

A number of faculty at the University of Minnesota gave generous assistance. Prof. Edwin Emery helped guide and encourage the historical research; Prof. Paul Murphy made me especially cognizant of the importance of asking "Why?" when analyzing historical data; Prof. Everette Dennis's encouragement and his own interests first stimulated my interest in this topic; and Prof. Phillip Tichenor provided advice in construction of the questionnaires. To Prof. Donald Gillmor I owe an inestimable debt, and not merely for his guidance and incisive criticism of this project. His intellectual discipline and unyielding standards and expectations gave me a vision of excellence I had not experienced before.

At Colorado State University, Prof. Don Zimmerman and Prof. Oguz Nayman gave freely of their time and expertise to advise me in constructing the final version of the survey questionnaires, developing the computer-coding scheme, solving computer problems, analyzing the data and refining the tables. Prof. Kenneth Berry also provided valuable help.

I certainly must thank Lynn, my wife, who was selflessly patient with me through five jobs, four moves and five years of graduate work. How she has put up with me, I shall never understand.

Finally, I want to dedicate this project to my mother and father. My mother typed the first version of the manuscript, but that is a small part of her overall contribution. So this is for you, Mom and Dad. You've given me more than I can ever return.

1

Introduction

Criticism of press coverage of the American judicial system is hardly a recent phenomenon. In the mid-nineteenth century, a disgruntled American journalist bitterly complained that

> the newspapers of the United States unwarrantably interfere with the administration of public justice; . . . they make it impossible for any man charged with a criminal offense to have a fair trial; . . . they have often caused the most desperate offenders to be acquitted and turned loose on society; and . . . many innocent persons, by their unwise or malicious meddling, have been brought to condemnation and punishment.[1]

More recently, the U.S. Supreme Court has been called the worst-reported institution in American government,[2] and coverage of the Court has been called inept and abominable.[3] A judge has noted that

> a good daily prints an average of two to five pages of sports, regularly, and in its own separate section, while court news may total less than one page with the stories scattered throughout the paper and hard to find. The comparative coverage may be symbolic of our values and our attitude, and—if this is as meaningful as might be inferred—it may also be symptomatic of something wrong with not only our press but our society.[4]

Despite the criticism heaped on the press by bench and bar, by scholars, by lay persons and by the press itself, our knowledge of the fundamental process through which court proceedings become news, particularly at the trial court level, is relatively meager—strikingly meager compared with our knowledge of the news-making process in other branches of government. How did court reporting originate and develop? What is the nature of the reporter-source interaction that produces court news? How do reporters and judicial sources perceive the role of the press? Does news making in the courts differ from news making in other branches of government? These and other questions have barely been touched. It is the purpose of this study to address such questions at the trial court level.

1

This chapter begins by sketching the type of criticism which has been leveled at media court reporting. It then specifies why the research which follows is needed and useful. The fundamental research questions are raised, the boundaries of the work are laid out, and the method is described.

CRITICISM OF COURT COVERAGE

The media and formal education are the public's principal sources of information about the courts.[5] Presumably, the very least the media should give the public is immediate information on what the courts are doing on a day-to-day basis, while formal education generally provides broader, more timeless information on the structure and processes of the judicial branch. But a recent national poll indicates that 70 percent of the general public either strongly agree or somewhat agree that the media should play an "important role in showing how the court system really works," and 71 percent either strongly or somewhat agree that the media should play an "important role in showing if the court system is effective."[6] Yet about half the respondents said media coverage is inadequate to show either how the system works or whether it is effective.[7]

That same national study found that the level of the general public's and community leaders' confidence in the courts is low; that the level of the general public's knowledge about courts is low; and, ironically, that those having the most knowledge and experience with courts were the most dissatisfied and critical—a finding which the pollsters say contrasts sharply with research on other organizations and institutions.[8] Among the respondents' complaints about the courts: The courts are too expensive; judges don't put in a full day's work and show little interest in people's problems; lawyers are too expensive and are interested more in themselves than in their clients.[9] Overall, 37 percent of the general public indicated having only slight or no confidence in state and local courts as institutions. (Thirty-three percent indicated slight or no confidence in the media.)[10]

Such findings only confirm what many have felt to be the case for some time. Grey, in his study of the news media and coverage of appellate courts, concluded that communication breaks down between the Supreme Court and both interested and mass publics, and he blamed both press and bar.[11] Sobel, too, has blamed low levels of public knowledge and understanding of the Supreme Court on the media and the Court; he complained that people rarely know exactly what the Court has held, why and with what consequences.[12] Similar criticism has been raised at the trial court level. For example, a study of media coverage of courts in Washington, D.C., concluded that although the courts deal with extremely important issues, the public understands less about the judiciary's operation, problems and needs than about those of the executive and legislative branches.[13] Peltason suggests that this may be due to the media and public having a different perception of the courts—a perception which leads to the belief that treating judges the same as legislators by analyzing their actions is somehow improper.[14] Not surprisingly, then, a survey in Maryland of judges, clerks, attorneys and reporters found that 90 percent of the respondents felt the courts needed to improve their image.[15]

One common thread underlying these criticisms and concerns is the idea that the press is a crucial link between judiciary and public, and that the right kind of press coverage can improve the public image and understanding of the courts. Thus some criticism and scholarship has considered the nature of the journalistic product itself. For example, Ericson analyzed the contents of three newspapers' coverage of the U.S. Supreme Court's October 1974 term and concluded that even a reader relying on the *New York Times* "would not know what really happened in more than three-fourths of the Court's decisions . . . not to mention why it happened and with what consequences for the reader."[16] Hachten studied how the press reported the 1962 school prayer decision and concluded that the press deserved some blame for public and even official misunderstanding of the decision.[17] Newland reached a similar conclusion in a study of the entire October 1961 term.[18] Meanwhile, Drechsel, Netteburg and Aborisade examined local trial court reporting in Minnesota newspapers and found that during a one-month period 20 percent of the county seat newspapers reported no local court action at all. Much of the rest of the reporting, they found, was simply lists of case dispositions.[19] Others, Grey and Center, for example, have criticized the press for concentrating on superficial issues, personalities and often uninformed reactions to decisions.[20]

This line of criticism often leads to a questioning of journalists' qualifications for handling complex legal issues. Hale studied wire service reporters covering a state supreme court and found that although none had taken any formal courses in law, none viewed this as a serious handicap.[21] Drechsel, after surveying nonmetropolitan daily newspaper court reporters in Minnesota and asking them about their education and experience, concluded that those who criticize reporters' qualifications for covering higher courts might have even a stronger case against those covering lower-level courts.[22]

Center was wrestling with this perceived problem more than 40 years ago as he pleaded for teaching journalism students about the legal process and how to understand it.[23] MacDougall expressed similar concerns when he published a 713-page textbook in 1946 to guide journalists in covering courts. "If we are to keep pace with the need for experts in all fields that provide news," he wrote in the preface, "we must have specialized books of reference and instruction."[24] Clearly, concerns about journalists' qualifications remain. In an article generally critical of news media coverage of *Herbert* v. *Lando*, a libel decision which the press generally perceived as a serious setback, Franklin worried that

> journalism education has traditionally failed to teach its students the realities of legal developments that greatly affect the media. Although the situation may be changing, most of those controlling the media today do not have the background to understand critical aspects of the judicial process.[25]

Lack of qualifications can have severe ramifications for court reporting. Hale's work suggests that reporters are unable to distinguish important questions of law at the appellate court level, even though law rather than facts is the major issue in appellate proceedings.[26] Obviously, the same could be true at the trial court level.[27] And attorney Whitney North Seymour has worried that if reporters do not understand how the judicial system works, they cannot possibly ask questions which might expose its weaknesses.[28] Consequently, he accuses the press of contributing to conditions which foster injustice.[29]

To summarize: Media coverage of the judicial branch has been criticized for failing to give the public the amount and type of information it needs to understand and to evaluate critically the judiciary. Coverage has also been criticized as frequently superficial if not misleading or inaccurate. Journalists themselves have been criticized for being inadequately trained in law and the judicial process and for therefore being unable to separate the significant from the sensational, unable competently to monitor the judiciary and unable to understand what they are observing and recording.

The fair trial–free press conflict is acknowledged but not directly considered by this study. The conflict does, however, have implications for reporter-source research. First, voices in the fair trial–free press debate acknowledge that the press may play a role in the judicial decision-making process, at least when juries are involved; second, those voices imply that sources may purposely give information to reporters in exchange for publicity beneficial to their sides in legal disputes. Both of these implications receive more extensive treatment in the following chapter.

It is important to note, however, that most of the criticism of press interference with impartial judicial decision making, particularly in jury cases involving felonies, is based on exceptional cases. It has not been grounded in discussion about routine day-to-day coverage of the courts, but in the coverage of particularly unusual or sensational, highly publicized cases. Much other criticism has been anecdotal or impressionistic. What scholarly study has been undertaken of reporter-source interaction in the judicial sphere has been done primarily at the appellate court level. Little work has been done at the trial court level, and it has been more descriptive than theoretical. In other words, despite the highly visible conflict between the constitutional values of fair trial and free press and despite the criticism of press coverage of the courts generally, we know pitifully little about the nature of routine reporter-source interaction—the news-making process—that creates the product which is so often deplored. And despite the fact that the fair trial–free press issue most directly affects the trial courts, we know least of all about the news-making process in these courts. This study attempts to fill some of that knowledge gap.

There are other reasons for this exploration. For one, it is with the trial courts that most citizens have their only direct contact. Thus local trial courts have the most direct and visible impact. At the same time, the only major sources of information about those courts' activities are the citizens who use them (or are forced to use them) and the local press. Assuming that litigants and attorneys will often be dissatisfied because of unfavorable outcomes, they are unlikely to be objective sources as they spread their news by personal communication.[30] A more reliable and balanced source of information about the local judiciary ought to be the local press. If an informed public is indeed the foundation of a democratic system, then how the local press covers courts may be a crucial determinant of public support for the judicial branch. Thus it is important to understand more about how that coverage comes about.

It has also frequently been asserted that the press plays a necessary and sometimes crucial role in government policy making, particularly in the legislative and executive branches. That role has influenced the nature of reporter-source interaction because it has given the press control of a commodity which many officials need and want—publicity. Therefore, a mutually beneficial situation has developed in which reporters and sources can exchange information and publicity. The role of the press in judicial policy making has received much less attention. If, as this study suggests, the role of the press in the judicial branch is different from that it plays in other branches of government, reporter-source relationships—and consequently the news-making process itself—ought to be affected.[31]

QUESTIONS FOR RESEARCH

Several broad research questions are considered in this study.

1. What insight into judicial news making and press-judiciary relations can be gained by considering the historical origins and development of trial court reporting?
2. What generalizations can be made about the news-making process in the trial courts?
3. Is the news-making process different in the trial courts than in other branches of government, and, if so, what implications might this difference have?

These questions are approached through a study of the historical development of newspaper court reporting in the United States and by a study of reporter-source interaction in state trial courts in Minnesota. The research attempts to build on the existing literature of reporter-source interaction, and may in part be seen as an exploration of how far generalizations from that literature may be fruitfully applied to news making in the trial courts.

The study is limited to newspaper coverage because such factors as time and space differences among media would make a more comprehensive approach difficult if not impractical. Further, the broadcast media, for example, generally do not assign beat reporters to trial courts, a fact not conducive to study of regular or routine reporter-source interaction. And many of the broadcast media are not primarily in the news business anyway.

The study is limited to courts of original jurisdiction—trial courts—in part because so little is known about routine reporter-source interaction there, in part because the trial courts receive the most spot news attention and in part because there are simply more trial courts than appellate courts and they are therefore more easily available to reporters. In Minnesota these courts include the state district courts, county courts and municipal courts.[32] The Minnesota study is limited to state trial courts— as opposed to the federal trial courts—because the state courts generate the most court coverage, they are located throughout the state and are therefore accessible directly to the largest number of reporters.[33] It must be conceded, of course, that limiting the study to courts and newspapers in Minnesota may limit the ability to generalize the results.

The study includes newspaper coverage of all aspects of the state trial courts, including their handling of any civil or criminal action from the time a case first comes to court until the trial courts finally dispose of the case. It considers spot news and feature coverage, but it does not consider editorial comment in letters to the editor or in newspapers' formal editorials and columns. It focuses on routine, day-to-day coverage, not on the coverage of particular cases only. And it considers primarily local coverage of local courts because the author is interested in recurring interaction between sources and reporters, not in the occasional appearance by an out-of-town reporter attracted by an unusual case of interest to a wider audience. It should be noted, too, that by considering the entire range of court activity—civil, criminal and other—the research goes beyond most of the existing literature which has been interested primarily in the fair trial–free press ramifications of criminal case coverage.

Finally, this study should be distinguished from the literature directed at the impact of press coverage on juries (again, primarily in criminal cases). It is only indirectly interested in the effects press coverage might have on juries. That is, this is a study of the news-making process, not a study of the consequences of the published product of that process. The effects of the product are of interest only to the degree that reporter-source interaction might be affected by reporters' and sources' beliefs about them. For example, a source might cooperate with a reporter because he or she believes publicity might influence the outcome of a case to his or her liking. But whether that result actually occurs is outside the scope of this study.

The study uses historical research, a case study and survey research. The historical research examines the origins and development of newspaper trial court reporting from its English roots to twentieth-century America. Secondary sources are used to study English origins and also to study court reporting in the United States. But for the study of court reporting in the United States, a sample of issues of several American newspapers is examined.

The case study is based on direct observation of a full-time court reporter for a metropolitan daily newspaper in Minnesota.

The survey research involved a questionnaire survey of state court judges, court clerks, attorneys and daily newspaper reporters in Minnesota. They were asked about the nature of their interaction and about some of their attitudes about the role of the press in reporting trial courts.

Each method is described in more detail in subsequent chapters. Chapter 2 examines the literature of reporter-source interaction and relates it specifically to such interaction in trial courts. Chapter 3 considers the historical development of newspaper court reporting. Chapter 4 presents the observational case study, and chapters 5 and 6 present the survey research. Chapter 7 briefly pulls together the findings, considers their major implications and suggests some directions for further research.

Notes

1. Lambert A. Wilmer, *Our Press Gang* (Philadelphia: Lloyd, 1859, Arno reprint, 1970), p. 52.

2. Max Freedman, "Worst Reported Institution," *Nieman Reports* 10 (April 1956): 2.

3. Philip B. Kurland, "On Misunderstanding the Supreme Court," *University of Chicago Law School Record* 9 (1960):31.

4. James O. Monroe, Jr., "Press Coverage of the Courts," *Quill*, March 1973, p. 24.

5. *The Public Image of Courts: Highlights of a National Survey of the General Public, Judges, Lawyers and Community Leaders* (Williamsburg, Va.: National Center for State Courts, 1978), p. 2.

6. Ibid., p. 13.

7. Ibid. Secondary schools have also been criticized for poorly educating students about the judicial system. See, e.g., "Judiciary Kicks Off Campaign to Close Education Gap," *Rocky Mountain News*, 8 June 1981, p. 6.

8. Ibid., p. ii. A study a decade earlier in Wisconsin found that a large portion of the general public watched or read about courts, but that their attention had little impact on their perceptions of the courts. Herbert Jacob, "Judicial In-

sulation—Elections, Direct Participation, and Public Attention to the Courts in Wisconsin," *Wisconsin Law Review* 1966 (Summer): 816. Jacob also concluded that public attention to the courts appears motivated by a desire for entertainment, and that news about trials and dramas about the courtroom have "the same political impact as the 'Dear Abby' column in the newspaper." Ibid., p. 818.

9. *Courts Image*, p. 49.

10. Ibid., p. 25. This finding squares with that of a 1978 Gallup Poll which found that only 19 percent of the residents of American cities of 50,000 or more gave a highly favorable rating to courts. See George H. Gallup, ed., *The Gallup Poll: Public Opinion 1978* (Wilmington, Del.: Scholarly Resources, 1979), p. 117.

11. David L. Grey, "Public Communication of U.S. Appellate Court Decisions" (Ph.D. dissertation, University of Minnesota, 1966), p. 463.

12. Lionel S. Sobel, "News Coverage of the Supreme Court," *American Bar Association Journal* 56 (June 1970):548. For criticism of the press for failing to examine the administrative side of the Supreme Court, see Everette E. Dennis, "How the Press Fails the Supreme Court," *Christian Science Monitor*, 21 February 1979, p. 22.

13. Community Education Committee of the Young Lawyers Section of the District of Columbia Bar Association, *The News Media and the Washington, D.C., Courts: Some Suggestions for Bridging the Communications Gap* (Washington, D.C.: News Media and Courts Committee of the Young Lawyers Section of the American Bar Association, 1972), p. 19.

14. Jack W. Peltason, *Federal Courts in the Political Process* (New York: Random House, 1955), p. 25.

15. Deborah Unitus Bereznak, "Public Information Needs Concerning Maryland's Courts—An Assessment" (Annapolis, Md.: Administrative Office of the State Courts, 1979), p. 12.

16. David Ericson, "Newspaper Coverage of the Supreme Court: A Case Study," *Journalism Quarterly* 54 (Autumn 1977):607. Of course, this may be better than what we know about what Congress is doing. See, e.g., Michael J. Robinson and Kevin R. Appel, "Network News Coverage of Congress," *Political Science Quarterly* 94 (Fall 1979):407–18; and Stephen Hess, *The Washington Reporters* (Washington, D.C.: Brookings Institution, 1981), pp. 105–107. For a more sanguine view of media coverage of the Supreme Court, see Michael E. Solimine, "Newsmagazine Coverage of the Supreme Court," *Journalism Quarterly* 57 (Winter 1980):661–63. Solimine compares his results with Ericson's.

17. William A. Hachten, "Journalism and the Prayer Decision," *Columbia Journalism Review*, Fall 1962, pp. 4–9.

18. Chester A. Newland, "Press Coverage of the United States Supreme Court," *Western Political Quarterly* 17 (March 1964):15–36. For a more recent analysis, see David Shaw, "Supreme Court Decisions Often Misinterpreted," *Los Angeles Times*, 11 November 1980, p. 3.

19. Robert Drechsel, Kermit Netteburg and Bisi Aborisade, "Community Size and Newspaper Reporting of Local Courts," *Journalism Quarterly* 57 (Spring 1980):74.

20. David L. Grey, "Covering the Courts: Problems of Specialization," *Nieman Reports* 26 (March 1972):17; Harry B. Center, "What Law Should the Reporter Know?" *Journalism Bulletin* 4 (March 1927):12. See also David Shaw, "Legal Issues: Press Still Falls Short," *Los Angeles Times*, 11 November 1980,

p. 1. For documentation of how relatively few interpretive stories are written by law reporters in Washington, D.C., see Hess, p. 110, n. 38.

21. F. Dennis Hale, "How Reporters and Justices View Coverage of a State Appellate Court," *Journalism Quarterly* 52 (Spring 1975):107.

22. Robert E. Drechsel, "How Minnesota Newspapers Cover the Trial Courts," *Judicature* 62 (October 1978):200. In fact, two recent studies have found reporters covering the U.S. Supreme Court to have considerable graduate school and law school training. See Everette E. Dennis, "Another Look at Press Coverage of the Supreme Court," *Villanova Law Review* 20 (1974–75):792; and Hess, pp. 53, 59.

23. "What Law Should the Reporter Know?"

24. Curtis D. MacDougall, *Covering the Courts* (New York: Prentice-Hall, 1946), p. vii. MacDougall's path has now been followed by Lyle W. Denniston, *The Reporter and the Law* (New York: Hastings House, 1980).

25. Marc A. Franklin, "Reflections on Herbert v. Lando," *Stanford Law Review* 31 (July 1979):1054. Franklin also worries that when smaller publications report on legal issues, they are particularly likely to misunderstand. Ibid., p. 1055. For a more optimistic view of media competence in legal reporting, see Shaw, "Legal Issues," p. 1.

26. Hale, p. 110.

27. Drechsel, p. 201.

28. Whitney North Seymour, Jr., *Why Justice Fails* (New York: William Morrow & Co., 1973), p. 204.

29. Ibid., p. 201. Seymour also believes sound coverage of the judiciary is important because there is no built-in two-party watchdog system in the judicial branch.

30. Jurors, witnesses, judges, clerks and spectators might be other personal sources of court information.

31. The literature of reporter-source interaction is considered in detail in the following chapter.

32. Minnesota also has conciliation, or small claims, courts, which might be considered courts of original jurisdiction, but which handle cases rather informally and which deal with relatively trivial disputes.

33. In Minnesota, the federal district courts sit permanently only in Minneapolis and St. Paul.

2

Reporters, Sources and Judicial News

To begin a study of news making in the trial courts, one must begin with the study of news making generally and the study of beat or specialized reporting particularly. Fortunately, the past two to three decades have seen the beginnings of a substantive, scholarly literature examining the news-making process. It is with that literature that this chapter begins. After considering the literature on news making in nonjudicial settings, the chapter examines the literature on news making in the courts—primarily the appellate courts. This literature is then used as a foundation from which the present study is launched.

NONJUDICIAL SOURCES AND REPORTERS

I begin with the assumption that news is less discovered than created by journalists. That is not to say that news is fabricated or made up. Good journalists don't make up facts. They do, however, select facts—or more often, they select facts "created" for them by individuals or bureaucracies. News, then, is created in the sense that what journalists offer as reality to readers is in fact a reality constructed in part by the journalist's sources and in part by the journalist's selection of some sources and not others. Or, as Lester has explained it: "newsworthy happenings do not lie 'out there.' The newsworthy character of happenings is constituted in and through the ways in which newsworkers of all sorts address happenings."[1]

There is nothing necessarily pernicious about this, but it does have implications. For example, although much news originates in bureaucracies—most frequently, government agencies—those sources have been producing their own versions of reality, "an idealized account of what agency officials want to happen, need to happen, and continually try to make happen."[2] Journalists can then turn "bureaucratic reality" into what readers may perceive to be a broader reality.[3] The same could be said about "facts" gathered from many individuals. Of course, that many sources have selfish or self-serving purposes is no surprise to journalists. To no small degree, the concepts of objectivity, balance and fairness are designed to meet that problem.

What may be less generally recognized is the degree to which the news is a result of a relatively restricted group of sources and the perspective imposed by the beat system of news gathering. The result is that some versions of reality are reported as news while others are not. Thus Gans, for example, has concluded that in the United States

> for the most part, the news reports on those at or near the top of the hierarchies and on those, particularly at the bottom, who threaten them, to an audience, most of whom are located in the vast middle range between top and bottom.[4]

Gans has also noted the difficulty he believes reporters have when called on to deal with sources who are at a social or even an ideological distance from them.[5] The converse is the relative ease with which reporters can deal with sources on beats, one result of which can be co-optation by those sources.[6]

To some degree, either explicitly or implicitly, these concepts—news as constructed reality, reliance on official sources, implications of beat reporting—appear in most reporter-source studies. Other generalizations may also be drawn, but they will be addressed later.

The roots of serious thinking about news making are traceable at least to Lippmann's *Public Opinion*, published in 1922.[7] Much of what he wrote then can be applied particularly to beat reporting. His seminal discussion of the working of stereotypes is reflected in analyses which suggest that beat reporters may tend to "define first and then see."[8] His thinking may also be detected in Tuchman's rather obtuse expression of her concern that

> typifications [of news events as "hard," "soft," etc.] can be seductive if objectified. Having a collective stock of knowledge-at-hand concerning how occurrences unfold and a system of typification partially based in the utility of known-in-detail prediction, news-workers may predict inaccurately.[9]

Lippmann also suggested that the press can normally record only what has been recorded for it by institutions and that "everything else is argument and opinion."[10] One might dispute that conclusion on several grounds, but as a description of what the press in fact does, it remains substantially accurate.

The first study to examine specifically the news-making process was Rosten's 1937 study of Washington correspondents.[11] Rosten focused on the reporters, not on the precise nature of their interaction with sources. Nevertheless, it was a useful beginning.[12] Another 20 years passed before Rosten's line of research was revived with Douglass Cater's *The Fourth Branch of Government* in 1959.[13] Subsequently, more than a dozen studies have addressed reporter-source interaction in the news-making process. These studies have examined coverage of Congress, federal agencies, state legislatures and agencies, and city government.[14]

Taken together, the studies suggest the following generalizations:

1. News making is not a simple, mechanical process. It is a rather complex sociopolitical process often involving actors in several bureaucracies.
2. The press, ergo, the news, plays an important role in government policy formation.
3. Reporters and sources can be classified into several general role types.

Each is worth closer scrutiny.

NEWS MAKING AS A SOCIOPOLITICAL PROCESS

News making is a social process because news is determined by and created through the interaction of individuals, groups, organizations and institutions. It can be called a political process because it involves the exercise of power and the distribution of rewards (and sometimes punishments). The social and political aspects of news making are closely linked, because the nature of the interaction is influenced by the power held by the participants. Thus Gieber and Johnson, in an early study of reporter-source interaction in city government, concluded that reporters and sources were members of different bureaucratic structures but cooperated in terms of their assigned communication roles. But their degree of mutual purpose and cooperation could at any given time be preempted by their respective social systems.[15] Sources used what resources they could to assimilate reporters and ultimately reporters tended to be co-opted.[16] Thus Sigal concludes that much news is really the product of the coupling of two information-processing machines—news organizations and government—and that "what newsmen report may depend less on who they are than on how they work."[17]

Making news, in other words, is a two-way street. The source holds information to which the reporter may not otherwise have access—at least easy, convenient, quick and timely access. The reporter can provide publicity the source may desire for personal or organizational reasons. Comparing this situation to a dance, Gans suggests that "although it takes two to tango, either sources or journalists can lead, but more often than not, sources do the leading."[18] Nevertheless, sources hardly have automatic open access to reporters.[19] Rather, their successful access to reporters and therefore to the media may differ according to their power, their ability to supply suitable information and their geographic and social proximity to journalists.[20]

What emerges, then, appears to be fundamentally an exchange model in which what becomes news depends in large part on the nature of the exchange transactions between reporters and sources. At the most general level, this exchange might be characterized as a trading of information or access to information for publicity or legitimation for the source,[21] or as "a product of...mediation by communicators who in turn are influenced by psychological and social forces."[22] At a more specific level, a routine news source might offer newsworthy information to a reporter because doing so makes him or her feel useful to the public or because the reporter has become an interesting friend or for any number of specific reasons.

The exchange concept is explicit or implicit in most of the reporter-source studies. But it has been criticized, most notably by Tunstall who points out that in many cases neither sources nor reporters can more than partially withdraw from the information-publicity exchange since there is not always an open market with many alternate sources or reporters.[23] He adds that most exchange models "ignore the instability of news, the loosely structured (or chaotic) character of the social interaction, and especially the lack of time for care, gradualness or full communication about the dispositions of different parties relevant to the rapidly changing 'current' story."[24]

To some degree, Tunstall is right. Certainly, exchange behavior cannot provide a complete explanation for the news-making process. Yet it is undeniable that exchange behavior occurs and occurs frequently. Further, the process may be more subtle than Tunstall suggests. First, the fact that the participants do not in every case consciously and purposely exchange information and publicity doesn't mean exchange is not occurring. Sigal, for example, has argued that, although what becomes news depends largely on journalists' choices, these choices needn't result from any highly conscious or formal weighing of issues.[25] Yet Sigal also suggests that in a larger sense, government sources give reporters information because of the strategic value publicity can have for them. Second, as noted above, exchange behavior can be addressed in a more specific sense. That is, the reporter may have more than just publicity to offer in exchange for information, and sources may have more to offer than information. For example, a reporter's exchange resources might include his or her friendship, or gossip that comes from other sources, or even ideas the reporter has about things important to a source. A source in turn might offer the reporter friendship or the status that accompanies being the intimate of a particular source.[26]

This discussion of exchange behavior leads to the next generalization that has emerged from reporter-source studies—that the press plays an important role in policy formation.

THE PRESS AND POLICY MAKING

Cater was among the first to explicitly and comprehensively address the role of the press in the federal government. He argued that "as broker and middleman" among the subgovernments of Washington, D.C., the reporter helps shape the course of government:

> He [the reporter] can choose from among the myriad events that seethe beneath the surface of government; which to describe, which to ignore. He can illumine policy and notably assist in giving it sharpness and clarity; just as easily, he can prematurely expose policy and, as with an undeveloped film, cause its destruction. At his worst, operating with arbitrary and faulty standards, he can be an agent of disorder and confusion. At his best, he can exert a creative influence in Washington politics.[27]

Reporters, in other words, can influence—by the very nature of their work—government decision making. They do so by constructing the reality (via the news) on which policy-makers may act and to which policy-makers react; by serving as perceived representatives of public opinion, thus helping define what is politically desirable and feasible for policy-makers; by focusing attention, thus influencing policy-makers' priorities; and by serving as a communication link between policy-makers and between sometimes competing bureaucracies.[28]

From the official's perspective, this influence can operate in both a reactive and anticipatory sense. That is, the press can influence policy making because officials react to what they see and hear in the media or because they act on the basis of anticipated media attention. Thus even if the media ultimately pay no attention to a source, the source may still act on the premise that attention might be forthcoming. Therefore, even if the press were to try to eschew any policy-making role, that would be impossible. As Nimmo concluded in his study of federal government information officers and the press, reporters and sources are "inextricably ensnarled in politics."[29]

This policy-making role of the press has been recognized by a series of reporter-source studies since Cater's, and at several levels of government.[30] Nevertheless, one might still surmise that not all reporters and sources will perceive their roles in precisely the same way. Indeed, one might expect some uneasiness over the situation. Thus we turn to the third generalization emerging from the reporter-source literature—that reporters and sources can be classified into several general role types.

REPORTERS, SOURCES AND ROLES

At least four major studies have specifically addressed the concept of reporter and/or source roles in nonjudicial government settings.[31] These are
the works by Cohen, Dunn, Nimmo and Hilton. They form the basis of
the following discussion.

As Cohen studied reporters covering foreign policy, he concluded
that they fell into two basic categories—neutral and participant. The
neutral-reporter type tended to put the burden of creating news onto
others, deferring in news judgment to colleagues, editors and sources.
The participant type, by contrast, used more independent criteria for determining newsworthiness, and often his or her concept of newsworthiness lay in notions about society rather than in the parade of ongoing
events.[32]

Dunn, in his study of state government officials and reporters, also
found two basic types—participant and nonparticipant reporters. The
nonparticipant reporters, he concluded, fell into three basic role types:
neutral transmitters of information; interpreters or translators of government information; or representatives of the public working as watchdogs,
exposers of secrecy and determiners of veracity.[33] The reporter in the role
of participant, on the other hand, might actually precipitate action or
work to focus attention on or exacerbate conflict. Such reporters, he
found, might go so far as to directly advocate policy in any number of
ways—by the attention they gave to some issues, by choosing carefully
which sides and sources to emphasize, by writing columns or analysis
pieces, and even in direct encounters with officials.[34] Dunn believes that
reporters are inherently pushed toward the participant role because that
role is actually the most functional for the goals of the reporter, while the
others are more abstractly functional for society.[35] According to Dunn,
the social environment pushes reporters toward the participant role because officials will deliberately try to make reporters participate; because
officials control access to information, and by "playing along," the reporter can keep lines of access open; because reporters like to be well
thought of by high-status officials; and because just being around and becoming familiar with the system facilitates reporters' interest in making
policy.[36]

Nimmo identified three basic reporter roles in his study of federal
public information officers and the press. The "recorder" sees his job as
providing facts without opinion, is devoted to objectivity and is generally
a reporter of general news who has relatively less discretion in selecting
what to cover. The "expositor" is devoted to interpretation, can be more
selective in what he covers, isn't afraid to make his own views known and
is likely to be a specialist. The expositor often supplements the recorder.
The third type, the "prescriber," openly states what he believes has gone

right or wrong in government and freely suggests alternatives. He sees himself as articulator of public opinion, and as servant to both the public and the elite stratum of officials. To the prescriber, objectivity is not an important value.[37]

Hilton's analysis of reporter types shares some fundamental elements of the other three analyses, but as she defines them, she also addresses some of the ambivalence reporters may feel about these roles. To Hilton, the "politically oriented pro" is really interested in the political process, is an interpreter, a digger, a supplementer of spot news. In that respect, the politically oriented pro resembles Dunn's nonparticipants and Nimmo's expositors. But Hilton also notes that the politically oriented pro can't escape involvement in the events he reports, is aware of it but feels threatened by it because he has no desire to influence policy. Meanwhile, the "craft-oriented" reporter is governed by norms of speed and efficiency. He serves the "conveyor belt" function and is highly oriented toward spot news and objectivity. He has little sense of involvement. He resembles Cohen's neutral reporter, Dunn's neutral transmitter and Nimmo's recorder. Finally, Hilton isolates the "frustrated idealist," a reporter who is ambivalent about his role, a reporter who feels the craft-oriented pressure to conform to newsroom roles yet is frustrated because he feels socially responsible but sees no market for the kind of information a socially responsible reporter should be dispensing. The frustrated idealist strongly feels a conflict between objectivity and involvement.[38]

If reporters can be classified into role types, so can sources, and here the work of Nimmo is most explicit and useful. Just as he sees reporters acting as recorders, expositors and prescribers, he sees sources acting as informers, educators and promoters. The "informer" sees his or her task as reporting to the press and public factually without interpretation. The informer is not concerned with policy making or promotion and sees himself as servant of public, press and organization—in that order. The "educator" sees his or her task as providing interpretation which expands on facts to create understanding of policy but is not directed toward making policy decisions. And the "promoter" is oriented primarily toward the organization, actively helps with policy formation and is acutely aware of the value of timing and publicity.[39]

Combining the reporter and source roles, Nimmo finds that reporter-source relationships can be classified in three fundamental ways—as cooperative, compatible or competitive. The cooperative relationship is one in which relations are informal and friendly, communication is informal and continuous, both share views of each other's responsibilities, they tend to share common news judgment and tend to be fairly close friends. A compatible relationship breeds more tension but still there is harmony; communication is less regular and more formal; there is some disagreement about how each views the other's responsibilities; there is not total agreement on newsworthiness; and reporter and source are not such close friends. A competitive relationship is marked by a formal and untrusting atmosphere with infrequent and highly formal communication. Reporter and source disagree in their views of each other's responsibilities and on news judgment; in friendship terms, their relationship is distant.[40]

To illustrate: Recorders and informers are likely to have cooperative relationships; recorders and educators are likely to be compatible; prescribers and promoters are likely to be competitive.[41] Nimmo found the compatible relationship to be the most common between agency information officers and the press,[42] and he concluded that reporters and sources tend to "choose" each other in the degree to which they share the same sense of news values.[43] He also concluded that issues involving government secrecy and news management "are as much a reflection of these relationships as they are causes of them."[44]

At least one other implication of the study of reporter and source roles merits attention. Cohen points out that when reporters hold to an objective transmission of information perspective, they in effect hand the initiative to sources. Yet sources tend generally not to seek out reporters, so neither group wants to take responsibility for thorough, comprehensive news coverage and consequently much information is lost. This situation simultaneously enhances the influence of those in the government and press who do act as independent "inputters."[45] Nimmo expresses a similar concern—that the journalist is not willing to accept the responsibility for leadership which inheres in his definition of his role.[46]

To summarize, then, let us restate the basic generalizations emerging from the reporter-source literature: reporter-source interaction is sociopolitical in nature with reporters and sources acting in several possible roles. The outcome of this interaction is not only "news" but an influence on government decision making itself.[47] With this foundation, we can turn to a consideration of reporters and sources in the judicial system.

REPORTERS, SOURCES AND THE JUDICIARY

I begin with the assumption that news making in the judicial branch of government is no less a sociopolitical process than it is in other branches of government. That is not to say there are no differences, only that the fundamental process is the same. That assumption made explicit, I shall consider the reporter-source literature of the judicial branch, compare and contrast it with the reporter-source literature discussed above and then lay out in some detail the rationale for the research reported in the following chapters.

The first thing to become apparent from any examination of the literature of news making in the judicial branch is its scantiness, particularly at the trial court level. Although much of the work is only descriptive, several sound studies have been undertaken, and a number of them build on the theoretical work done in earlier reporter-source studies. Perhaps the most outstanding work has been done by Grey and Stanga. Grey studied how the news media cover federal appellate courts—primarily the U.S. Supreme Court.[48] Stanga studied how the criminal justice system was reported in three cities in Wisconsin.[49] Stanga's work is particularly relevant here because he used the foundation provided by Cohen and Dunn to construct a basic typology of criminal justice reporters and because he applied an exchange model to reporting which included court reporting.

Stanga classified his reporters as "informers" and "guardians." The former see the press as an intermediary between policy-makers and the electorate, and see their job as giving the public facts on which democratic evaluations of government performance can be based.[50] The latter perceive their job as overseeing government and guarding against government incompetence and misdeeds.[51] It is significant that these categories differ from Dunn's and Cohen's to the degree that Stanga's do not so clearly distinguish reporters who do and do not see themselves as participants in the policy-making process. Indeed, both of Stanga's categories seem to fit best into Dunn's nonparticipant roles. This suggests a difference between judicial and nonjudicial reporting (although Stanga's study encompassed a great deal of nonjudicial or noncourt reporting). That is, the press probably does not play the same policy-making role vis-à-vis the judiciary that it does in the other branches of government. That doesn't mean the press plays no role at all in judicial decision making, but the role might be substantially different. I shall return to this point later.

Stanga also analyzed reporter-source interaction using an exchange model, and he found the model to be useful. While he noted that a considerable amount of information in the judicial system is "free" because it is on the public record or comes from open court proceedings, reporters still need such things as added color or descriptive detail—particularly because reporters can't always be in the courtroom at the right time.[52] He also found that reporters frequently obtained information from lawyers, judges, police, clerks and others as to which court proceedings would be of value and which would not.[53] What did the participants exchange? In addition to such "commodities" as friendship, information and some ego-massage, Stanga found that the reporter's informer-role orientation itself was a commodity of exchange.[54] Thus it was quite possible for reporters to have informer orientations toward some sources and guardian orientations toward others.[55]

Other studies have more indirectly hinted that reporters and sources in the judiciary can be seen in particular roles. For example, one study of the news media and court coverage in Washington, D.C., found that while newsmen see their job in terms of "informing" the public, of obtaining and publishing the maximum possible amount of information for their readers and viewers, judges are more concerned with creating a calm and dispassionate atmosphere in which criminal prosecutions and disputes between citizens can be fairly and rationally adjudicated.[56]

And a manual for state court clerks in Minnesota reminds clerks that they "can play a significant role in educating the reporter on the workings of the court,"[57] advice which brings to mind Nimmo's "educator" source role. Then lest there be doubt that there may be a conscious or unconscious struggle for control between judicial sources and reporters, there is the statement of one court reporter about another: "She's almost more lawyer than reporter."[58]

If news making in the courts is fundamentally similar to news making in the legislative and executive branches of government, what role, if any, does the press play in judicial policy making?

Several writers have suggested that at a general level, the U.S. Supreme Court tends to follow public opinion, which it apparently senses in part through the news media. Gaziano, for example, found a statistical correlation between Supreme Court decisions on freedom of expression for deviant political groups and public opinion on that issue.[59] Funston has found support for the hypothesis that over long periods of time, the Supreme Court reflects the will of the dominant political forces, but that during periods of major political realignment, the Court will be more likely to perform countermajoritarian functions.[60] Casper has concluded that public opinion and the activities of other public institutions are crucial to understanding the "somewhat checkered path" followed by the Court in loyalty-security cases.[61]

Nevertheless, in a narrower sense and at a more specific level of analysis, declining support doesn't influence judicial policy as much as policy in other social and political systems.[62] In other words, if the press does affect judicial policy making or decision making, the effect is more subtle and indirect than the press's effect on other government policy making. Jacob, for example, believes this is so because with the courts, "public opinion must first be filtered through executive and legislative officials before it can constrain judicial action."[63] Goldman and Jahnige make a similar point, noting that media feedback probably has little immediate effect on judicial policy, but that such feedback is important indirectly because

> it both reflects and shapes public and political opinions. By its praise and criticism of specific Court outputs and general behavior, it provides vital inputs of information and opinion for politicians, public officials, interest group leaders, and even private citizens in determining their responses to judicial policymaking.[64]

Grey found that U.S. Supreme Court justices do use the news media for feedback.[65] Yet he concluded that "the press does affect the public image of what the Court has said, but there is little evidence of anything more than a transmission-of-information role."[66]

At the lower court level, Stanga began his work with the central thesis that journalists are participants in the criminal justice process.[67] Indeed, one of his conclusions was that in some cases police-prosecutor-newsman interactions did help determine the decision to file a charge. Yet he conceded that

> news coverage of the criminal justice system does not usually entail reporting policymaking innovations and the newsman's sphere of activity is in a sense more circumscribed than that of the political reporter.[68]

Eisenstein, too, has noted that state court judges have some fear of drawing censure from the local press.[69] He has also noted an influence on prosecutors. For example, if a crime attracts great publicity, the prosecutor feels little choice but to prosecute; he feels he must cultivate a general image of competence and effectiveness on routine cases by maintaining a high conviction rate:

> The fact that he thinks everyone is watching his conviction rate (whether they are or not) raises fears that a drop in the number or proportion of convictions would lead to public outcry, a ruined reputation, and damage to his future prospects in both law and politics.[70]

Although he notes that the precise impact is difficult to measure, Jacob agrees that the mere possibility of press attention structures the expectations and behavior of judicial decision-makers.[71]

If the press can even subtly influence the judicial policy-making process, there ought to be some evidence that actors in the judicial branch may try to influence the media. There is some such evidence, although it is extremely tenuous and merely suggestive. At the U.S. Supreme Court, Goldschlager concluded, the informal relationship that developed between the court's press officer and regular court reporters may have significantly affected the reporters' news judgment.[72] Goldschlager also concluded that the press officer was a "significant source of reinforcement for the status quo definition of what [was] newsworthy."[73] At the trial court level, an orientation manual for state court clerks in Minnesota urges clerks to do a good job on community relations because good relations can make the courts' job easier, foster a law-abiding atmosphere, affect the willingness of community members to appear as witnesses and jurors and build support for providing the courts with adequate resources.[74]

There are reasons why the press apparently plays a different, more subtle and more indirect role in the judicial branch than in the other branches of government. The courts' publicity needs are inherently different from those of the other branches. For one thing, courts are, at least in theory, supposed to decide cases on neutral principles after dispassionate consideration of arguments made by all parties under clearly specified ground rules. Obviously, it is open to dispute whether this is always what happens in practice. But the point is that the judiciary is expected to make its decisions differently from the legislative and executive branches. While the overt mobilizing of public and interest group support, response to pressure groups, decision making according to what a majority of one's constituents want, and political logrolling are taken to be the norm—whether approved of or not—in legislative and executive decision making, such activities are anathema to judicial decision making.[75] This fundamental difference has at least two major implications for the role of news media.

First, the press is not needed as a source of information on which judicial decisions are based, as an extraofficial communication channel linking one court with another or as an essential channel linking the judiciary with other government decision-makers. The courts are quite able to gather the information they need for decision making and to gather it more thoroughly and exhaustively than the press could. In part, this is because, unlike the other branches of government, the judiciary must wait for cases and controversies to come to it. Thus, for example, Congress or a state legislature might become involved in an issue after and because it has surfaced in the news media, and then respond in large part to the issue as it has been defined in the media. The same issue, on the other hand, might reach the courts in the form of a dispute between two parties, and be presented for a decision only after extensive voluntary and compelled discovery, legal research, testimony and argument by counsel. That issue might reach the courts regardless of whether it has first been attended to by the news media. Indeed, the information needed for judicial decision making may be far more specific and detailed than the media are likely to or able consistently to provide.[76]

Another reason the courts have relatively little need for the media as a source of information in decision making is the self-contained, specialized information system generated by the bench and bar. Judges base decisions on existing common and statute law and on some of the scholarly legal literature as they apply to the facts of a case. This system is easily accessible and decentralized throughout the nation. Judges and attorneys don't need reporters to tap this information and tell them about it. This also means that the media are not essential as communication links among judges or between bench and bar. As Grey noted in his study of the press and the appellate courts, lawyers and judges

> can ignore the media and still find out nearly all that has happened by reading the Court's formal record. Also, the law is a fairly slow process; the lawyer or judge can usually afford to wait to see the full record. There usually is little urgency to find out what the Court has decided; the law is there and will wait for the professionals until they need it in their work.[77]

Data gathered by Berkson bear this out. He found that of ten "specialized" publics surveyed, judges, attorneys and law enforcement officers relied least on newspapers, television, radio and general periodicals for reliable information about U.S. Supreme Court decisions. Instead, they tended to use specialized memoranda, bulletins and newsletters.[78]

The second general implication for the news media has to do with the need of the judiciary for a communication link with the general public. At first glance, it might seem as though the courts should most closely resemble the other branches of government when it comes to the need for a communication link with the public. In the most general sense, this is probably true. There are, after all, few alternative channels to the news media as a means of reaching the public. Thus it is not surprising that Johnson, in his study of compliance with the U.S. Supreme Court's school prayer decision, found that newspapers, radio, television and magazines were the principal means by which the word of what the Court had done filtered down to the community level.[79] Yet the courts have been remarkably indifferent to the importance of this communication link. Anthony Lewis is one of many to note that at the U.S. Supreme Court there is no public relations machinery.[80] What evidence there is indicates that unlike congressmen or legislators, judges seldom attempt purposely to use the media for either their personal or institutional benefit. There is no overt effort to use publicity to carefully mobilize or prepare public opinion for an upcoming judicial decision. And when such efforts—for example, by attorneys—are detected, they are soundly criticized both within and without bench and bar.

If there is any consciousness at all of the role of the news media, it most likely has to do with using the media to improve the public's image and understanding of the judiciary and to facilitate compliance with decisions with broader policy implications. Even in this realm, however, obvious examples are uncommon.

This failure of the judicial branch to place high value on publicity as a commodity would seem to have implications for the nature of the news-gathering process. If the courts generally do not value publicity as a commodity to be exchanged for information, what commodities does the reporter have to offer? There are still some: friendship, for example, or giving a judge or clerk the "satisfaction" of fulfilling a people's right to know, perhaps.

Of course, to some degree this situation can be reversed. That is, since most judicial information comes from public records and public proceedings, it might seem that reporters have relatively little need for judicial sources. But there are several reasons why this is not unqualifiedly true. First, there are myriad cases in the judicial system at all times, and the reporter's time is limited. The reporter therefore needs help in choosing what to cover and in finding out what he or she has missed observing firsthand. Second, the law is often complex and seemingly unintelligible.

Misunderstanding is easy for the untrained observer. The reporter needs sources to provide background and understanding, to explain the complexities, and against which to check interpretations.

In any case, although there will still be sociopolitical interaction between reporters and sources in the judiciary, the resources each brings to bear would seem to be different from those available in coverage of other branches of government. Therefore, the nature of reporter-source interaction in the judiciary ought to be somewhat different, and that is what the literature generally suggests.

One of the most striking findings of studies, particularly at the appellate court level, is the inaccessibility of judges as sources.[81] Newland, among others, has noted that press interviews with justices are rare at the U.S. Supreme Court and press conferences are nonexistent.[82] Ironically, this does not necessarily give journalists more editorial freedom from their sources. As Grey has pointed out, Supreme Court reporters actually have the Court's standards of news judgment imposed on them—that is, their news is defined by the legal issues and there is generally less room for interpretation.[83]

But there is evidence that accessibility increases as one descends the judicial hierarchy. Grey found federal appeals court justices to be more accessible and open than Supreme Court justices.[84] Hale found that although state supreme court justices in Washington had infrequent contact with the press, two-thirds of the justices said they would cooperate with reporters by explaining their own decisions or answering reporters' questions on general points of law.[85] Yet he also found that reporters were generally well satisfied with the cooperation of attorneys, justices and court officials, and felt that it would be improper to ask a judge for anything more than for-background-only explanation.[86]

At the trial court level there is also evidence of more accessibility and cooperation from judicial sources, although there is some contradictory evidence. Drechsel, in a study of nonmetropolitan daily newspaper court reporters in Minnesota, found that the reporters considered judges and court clerks to be cooperative sources. Private attorneys and public defenders were found to be the least cooperative.[87] In interviews with several metropolitan daily newspaper court reporters in Minnesota, Berg was told that judges and clerks were generally open and accessible. One reporter noted that she relied heavily on judges and attorneys to explain technical points of law and key issues in particular cases.[88] Another said that as she became better known to sources, "she was able to rely more on clerks, lawyers, and judges to identify important cases [and] now people recognize her, and may tip her off to unusual cases and stories."[89] Bereznak found that judicial sources in Maryland would generally respond to a reporter's questions on details of a specific case, but that court employees rarely volunteered information.[90] On the other hand, court clerks in Minnesota have been urged by top court administrators to go beyond helping reporters with hard news by suggesting ideas for feature stories or preparing news releases on court administration.[91] Yet a study of courts and news media in Washington, D.C., found that most District of Columbia judges and lawyers were very reluctant to grant interviews to reporters, that judges were wary of the media in all matters and that lawyers feared distortion.[92]

To summarize: Reporter-source interaction in the judicial branch, like that in other branches of government, is fundamentally a sociopolitical process. But the nature of the interaction seems to be different largely because the press appears to play a different role in its coverage of the judiciary than in its coverage of other branches of government. Court reporters and sources may usefully be categorized, and there is no reason to believe they do not engage in exchange behavior. But because the inherent value of publicity is not the same to actors in the judicial branch as to those in other branches, reporters must use different resources to obtain source cooperation.

A FOUNDATION FOR FURTHER STUDY

The following chapters build descriptively and theoretically on the base established by the scholarly work considered in this chapter. They consider the nature of judicial reporter-source interaction in the trial courts, the roles in which reporters and sources act and the reasons for which they cooperate.

Central to the theoretical basis of this study is the assumption that the news media play a different role in judicial policy making than in other government policy making, and that as a result the nature of reporter-source interaction ought to be affected. If so, it follows that if one uses an exchange model to consider the interaction, there ought to be less overt use of publicity for sources' personal reasons as an exchange commodity in the judicial branch than in other branches of government. That is, sources in the judicial system will cooperate with reporters primarily for reasons other than a personal need or desire for publicity (such as to increase personal leverage in the decision-making process).

This is not to say that sources will not cooperate at all for publicity reasons. Of course, some sources in the judicial system may well need publicity more than others, a situation which should be particularly true in the trial courts. Generally speaking, the trial courts are not constantly enmeshed in decision making with broad policy implications; rather, they are busy applying precedent and statute law to varying factual situations. That is, they are primarily applying policy made by higher courts or legislative bodies. In legal terms, they are making decisions as much on facts as on law. Appellate courts, on the other hand, focus on the law—or, one might say, on the policy being applied to facts. If lasting change is to be made in that policy, it must ultimately be made by the highest courts in the judicial hierarchy—a state supreme court, let us say. Therefore, it follows that if the judicial system generally has relatively less need than other branches of government for publicity in the policy-making process, that need should be least of all in the trial courts where broad policy is made the most seldom. Perhaps this is a logical point at which to distinguish more clearly the terms "policy making" and "decision making." In one sense they are identical: policy making requires decision making. Conversely, however, decision making does not necessarily involve the making of policy, although it may well involve the application or interpretation of policy. Thus at the trial court level, decision making is the more appropriate term. In any case, trial court judges would seem to have very little need for personal publicity in their decision making. Therefore, to them, there is relatively little need to exchange information with reporters for publicity. To the degree that they do desire publicity, it would seem most likely to be publicity to enhance the overall public understanding of and image of the trial courts in order to build a more favorable environment for acceptance of judicial decisions. The same reasoning ought to apply to court clerks, although, if anything, they should have even less a stake in such publicity than judges since clerks are often appointed, not elected.

Of course, some trial judges may aspire to the appellate bench or to other political offices. The evidence, however, suggests that judges may be less ambitious than one might expect. Eisenstein notes that federal judges generally regard their posts as the high point and end point of their careers.[93] He also concludes that while some elected lower court judges in state courts do move on to other government jobs, for many the bench is a terminal position.[94] If any argument is to be made regarding the movement of judges between the bench and other government jobs, it is that judges are more likely to come to the bench from a government job than to leave the bench for one.[95] Further, the evidence suggests that the trial court bench is not a clear stepping-stone to higher judicial office.[96]

Even if trial court judges do aspire to the appellate bench, there is little evidence that mass media coverage is vital to their success. This is especially true since the vast majority of judges are at least initially appointed, not elected, to office.[97] Grossman has noted that some candidates for federal judicial appointments do promote themselves but that they aim their "campaigns" at their senators or perhaps at the U.S. Justice Department, and do so quite privately.[98] Goldman concluded that federal appeals court judges gained appointment "largely due to fortuitous circumstances; they were in the right place at the right time. Many had contacts or friends with contacts."[99] Moreover, when potential candidates are screened, it is primarily their own judicial decisions and other writing that are studied, not news media accounts of them.[100] But even when accession to judicial office is via election, the media's role is questionable. Not only are people unlikely to vote in judicial elections, they are also likely to be hopelessly uninformed about issues and candidates.[101]

What about trial court judges' concern about reelection? Should this not be a significant reason for judges to need personal publicity from the media? The answer would appear to be "no." Compared to other elected officials, judges apparently need have few worries about retaining their positions. According to Eisenstein, "defeat of incumbent judges is so infrequent that as a practical matter, they can be thought of as appointees."[102] Nor is it unusual for judges to run unchallenged.[103] As Jacob concluded after studying judicial elections in Wisconsin, "elections do not seriously threaten the judge's tenure, force him to defend his decisions, or impose upon him the role of a partisan politician."[104] Apparently if there is any crucial factor in judicial elections, it is party label.[105] These factors, coupled with the general disinterest and ignorance of voters in judicial elections, lead to the conclusion that elections do not normally serve as feedback devices for the judiciary[106] and that the "conditions for direct control of [judges'] behavior through elections appear to be largely absent."[107]

Perhaps if any judicial source would be cognizant of the value of publicity for career advancement, it should be attorneys who might aspire to the bench or to other political office. In fact, there is evidence that criminal prosecutors, for example, do perceive their offices as potential stepping-stones.[108] For other reasons, too, attorneys might have tangibly more to gain than judges or clerks from the right kind of media publicity. But generalization is difficult. In some situations, for example, the criminal prosecutor might well desire publicity as an aid to conviction; in others, publicity might be dysfunctional. It might create sympathy for a defendant. The same is true for the criminal defense attorney. The situation is yet different for the attorney in civil practice. The press generally ignores civil actions unless broader policy implications or broader social effects are obvious. Therefore, there is less incentive for reporters to need these attorneys as sources, so even if such an attorney wanted to use publicity, he or she might be unsuccessful. Yet in civil cases to which the press does attend, the attorneys may or may not wish to have publicity. Their criterion for need—whether within or without the bounds of legal ethics—is likely to be what is best for a favorable outcome for the client.

Overall, however, if there is any group of sources commonly used by reporters in the judicial system who will be likely to see publicity as an important commodity, it is attorneys. However, the term "publicity" must be qualified. I shall use the word "manipulative," without intending any of the pejorative connotations the word may carry, simply to distinguish publicity that is welcome, sought and used primarily to attain more specific personal ends as opposed to more general, system-oriented ends. An example of manipulative publicity would be that desired because it might help an attorney win a case; an example of nonmanipulative public-ity would be that desired because it might increase general public under-standing of the judicial system. Such distinctions are useful in understand-ing the news-making process because they lead us back to consideration of the resources that sources and reporters bring to their interaction. Such considerations, in turn, can help us understand how and why judicial news is made.

Sources' reasons for cooperating are also linked to the concept of role types. Here Nimmo's categorization of sources as informers, educators and promoters is directly relevant. The presumedly lesser role of the press in judicial policy making suggests that promoter sources ought to be rel-atively rare and that when they do appear, they are more likely to be attorneys than judges or clerks. But it shouldn't be surprising even if rel-atively few attorneys fall into this role type. In any case, the role types into which sources and reporters fall have ramifications for the interaction between them, for the types of relationships they have and, ultimately, for the information that becomes news.

We must return, then, to the basic research questions this study poses about news making in trial courts. It is to those questions that the research in the following chapters turns.

Notes

1. Marilyn Jo Lester, "News as a Practical Accomplishment" (Ph.D. dis-sertation, University of California, Santa Barbara, 1974), p. 386.

2. Mark S. Fishman, "Manufacturing the News" (Ph.D. dissertation, Uni-versity of California, Santa Barbara, 1977), p. viii. Fishman's dissertation has sub-sequently been published as a book under the same title.

3. Ibid.

4. Herbert J. Gans, *Deciding What's News* (New York: Pantheon Books, 1979), p. 284. Gans's study is based primarily on participant observation of jour-nalists working for the "CBS Evening News," "NBC Nightly News," *Newsweek* and *Time*. He also used content analysis.

5. Ibid., p. 125.

6. Another result is that the same event may take on different forms when reported by journalists on different beats. For example, a court case involving a state trying to stop a large industry from dumping allegedly hazardous wastes into a stream might interest reporters on law, political and environmental beats. But the law reporter might see primarily the legal and factual issues involved, while the political reporter perceives the case as primarily a dimension of a political power struggle, while the environmental reporter considers the issue primarily in environmental terms. That is not to say that each reporter will be totally myopic; it is to suggest that each is likely to approach the story from a different perspec-tive. "A beat provides for a scheme of interpretation to pattern the features of a happening." Lester, p. 388.

7. Walter Lippmann, *Public Opinion* (New York: Macmillan, 1922).

8. Ibid., p. 81.

9. Gaye Tuchman, *Making News* (New York: Free Press, 1978), p. 59.

10. Lippmann, p. 361.

11. Leo C. Rosten, *The Washington Correspondents* (New York: Harcourt, Brace & Co., 1937).

12. For a partial replication of Rosten's study, see William L. Rivers, "The Correspondents after 25 Years," *Columbia Journalism Review*, Spring 1962, pp. 4–10. The most recent extensive study of journalists in Washington, D.C., who cover national government is Stephen Hess's *The Washington Reporters* (Washington, D.C.: Brookings Institution, 1981).

13. Douglass Cater, *The Fourth Branch of Government* (New York: Vintage, 1959).

14. Coverage of the judicial branch has also been studied, but those studies will be considered later in this chapter.

15. Walter Gieber and Walter Johnson, "The City Hall Beat: A Study of Reporter and Source Roles," *Journalism Quarterly* 38 (Summer 1961): 290.

16. Ibid., p. 297.

17. Leon V. Sigal, *Reporters and Officials: The Organization and Politics of Newsmaking* (Lexington, Mass.: D.C. Heath & Co., 1973), pp. 4–5.

18. Gans, p. 116.

19. Obviously, there are exceptions—the President of the United States, for example.

20. Gans, p. 117.

21. Fishman, p. 308.

22. Walter Gieber, "Two Communicators of the News: A Study of the Roles of Sources and Reporters," *Social Forces* 39 (1960):77.

23. Jeremy Tunstall, *Journalists at Work* (London: Constable, 1971), p. 186.

24. Ibid., p. 202.

25. Sigal, p. 2.

26. Perhaps this suggests one more reason why a source's status plays such an important role in news judgment. "Usually, the criteria for judging the news value of statements offered to the press are, first, the status of the source and, only secondly, the validity of the statement's content. Validity tends to become more important as a criterion of news value as the source's social rank declines." Bernard Roshco, *Newsmaking* (Chicago: University of Chicago Press, 1975), p. 50.

27. Cater, p. 7.

28. See, for example, Delmer D. Dunn, *Public Officials and the Press* (Reading, Mass.: Addison-Wesley, 1969), pp. 164–70.

29. Dan D. Nimmo, *Newsgathering in Washington* (New York: Atherton, 1964), pp. 42–43.

30. Sigal concluded that such an influence exists in the federal government generally and that officials disclose information largely "in an effort to muster and maintain support, both in and out of government, for a particular course of action." Sigal, p. 181. Cohen found a similar role for the press in the making of U.S. foreign policy, concluding that the press helps to create "common understandings or interpretations of political reality" for policy-makers. Bernard C. Cohen, *The Press and Foreign Policy* (Princeton: Princeton University Press, 1963), p. 246. Cohen also noted that reporters on their rounds carried policy thought from one interested source to another (p. 145); gave policy-makers a measure of the comparative importance of events in the eyes of others (p. 224); and

provided policy-makers with a measure of public opinion (p. 233). Chittick, studying the press and the state department, found that "the press is very important in providing Department officers with information about public opinion on foreign affairs." William O. Chittick, *State Department, Press and Pressure Groups* (New York: Wiley-Interscience, 1970), p. 182. In fact, he found that reporters actually felt they could influence department policy by reflecting public opinion, bringing opinions from lower- to upper-echelon officials, by questioning policy officers and as intermediaries between foreign emissaries and government officials. Ibid., p. 114. Nimmo examined interaction between journalists and information officers in the federal government and found that the "newsman performs an informal role as channel between the formal, impersonal levels of decisionmaking and the personal levels of citizen response and initiation." Nimmo, p. 210. Matthews concluded that reporters' definition of news influences senators' actions and helps define issues and that reporters are an essential communication link between senators and the outside world. Donald R. Matthews, *U.S. Senators and Their World* (Chapel Hill: University of North Carolina Press, 1960), p. 206. See also Robert O. Blanchard, ed., *Congress and the News Media* (New York: Hastings House, 1974). Dunn reached similar conclusions in his study of political reporters and state officials in Wisconsin, although he found that state officials seemed better able than federal officials to communicate with each other without the press. Dunn, pp. 15–16, 151. In a study of reporters and state legislators in Washington state, Hilton concluded that legislative reporters could hardly avoid becoming participants in the process because their very presence affects what happens in the legislative arena. Carol S. Hilton, "Reporting the Legislature: A Study of Newsmen and Their Sources" (M.A. thesis, University of Washington, 1966), p. 93. She found that legislators used the press to help them ascertain public opinion and to keep them apprised of developments in the other legislative chamber or in the other party. Some reporters even complained to Hilton that legislators frequently asked them how to vote. Ibid., pp. 93–94. Dyer and Nayman, in a study of reporters and legislators in Colorado, also found that many reporters considered themselves, at least in part, to be participants in the legislative process. Carolyn Stewart Dyer and Oguz B. Nayman, "Under the Capitol Dome: Relationships between Legislators and Reporters," *Journalism Quarterly* 54 (Autumn 1977): 452–53. Gieber and Johnson concluded that the city hall reporters they studied were actually a part of the city governmental process. Gieber and Johnson, p. 297. And Phillips, in a study that involved nearly 200 journalists in the Northeast, found that 85 percent of them believed they had written or supervised at least one story which had public policy impact. Barbara E. Phillips, "Approaches to Objectivity: Journalistic Versus Social Science Perspectives," in *Strategies for Communication Research*, eds. Paul M. Hirsch, Peter V. Miller and F. Gerald Kline (Beverly Hills: Sage Publications, 1977), p. 67. See also David Morgan, *The Capitol Press Corps: Newsmen and the Governing of New York State* (Westport, Conn.: Greenwood Press, 1978). For a British study, see Harvey Cox and David Morgan, *City Politics and the Press: Journalists and the Governing of Merseyside* (London: Cambridge University Press, 1973).

31. One major study involving the judiciary has used role analysis; it is examined in the text below.

32. Cohen, pp. 80–81. Johnstone et al. used Cohen's neutral-participant typology in their study of the characteristics of American journalists. John W. C.

Johnstone, Edward J. Slawski, and William W. Bowman, *The News People* (Urbana: University of Illinois Press, 1976), pp. 114–16.

33. Dunn, pp. 7–15.

34. Ibid.

35. Ibid. pp. 17–18. Sigal reaches a similar conclusion as he explains why independence from the newsroom means dependence on the beat. Sigal, p. 56.

36. Ibid.

37. Nimmo, pp. 48–53.

38. Hilton, pp. 123–40.

39. Nimmo, pp. 44–48. In some other studies, source roles are treated, but less directly. For example, Gieber found that sources of civil liberties news saw their role primarily as educators, not transmitters of information. Gieber, "Two communicators," p. 77.

40. Nimmo, pp. 211–17.

41. Ibid., p. 220.

42. Ibid., p. 219.

43. Ibid., p. 57.

44. Ibid., p. 208. Chittick implicitly suggests a related, if not similar, conclusion, when he finds that positional variables, not personal ones, are very important in explaining perceived antagonism among officials and reporters. Chittick, p. 211.

45. Cohen, p. 267.

46. Nimmo, pp. 221–22.

47. This is so despite the fact that study after study—including those by Gans, Dunn, Hilton, and Gieber and Johnson—has discovered that reporters have little specific, useful concept of audience. Yet a well-informed public is assumed to be the heart of a democratic system.

48. David L. Grey, "Public Communication of U.S. Appellate Court Decisions" (Ph.D. dissertation, University of Minnesota, 1966). This thesis became a book, Grey, *The Supreme Court and the News Media* (Evanston: Northwestern University Press, 1968).

49. John Ellis Stanga, Jr., "The Press and the Criminal Defendant: Newsmen and Criminal Justice in Three Wisconsin Cities" (Ph.D. dissertation, University of Wisconsin, 1971).

50. Ibid., p. 165.

51. Ibid., pp. 165–66.

52. Ibid., pp. 195–200.

53. Ibid., p. 200. Stanga concluded that official law enforcement sources, police and prosecutors were more important sources than defense attorneys and judges. Stanga, p. 292.

54. Ibid., p. 344.

55. Ibid., p. 173.

56. Community Education Committee of the Young Lawyers Section of the District of Columbia Bar Association, *The News Media and the Washington, D.C., Courts: Some Suggestions for Bridging the Communications Gap* (Washington, D.C.: News Media and Courts Committee of the Young Lawyers Section of the American Bar Association, 1972), p. 13.

57. Minnesota Continuing Education for State Court Personnel, *Minnesota Clerk of Court Manual* (St. Paul, 1977), p. 12.

58. Mary Joan Berg, "Who are the Newspaper Reporters—and What Do They Think?" *Hennepin Lawyer* 48 (November–December 1978):15.

59. Cecilie Gaziano, "Relationship Between Public Opinion and Supreme Court Decisions: Was Mr. Dooley Right?" *Communication Research* 5 (April 1978): pp. 131–49.

60. Richard Funston, "The Supreme Court and Critical Elections," *American Political Science Review* 69 (1975): 795–811.

61. Jonathan D. Casper, *The Politics of Civil Liberties* (New York: Harper & Row, 1972), p. 75. See also Beverly Cook, "Public Opinion and Federal Policy," *American Journal of Political Science* 21 (August 1977):567–600.

62. Sheldon Goldman and Thomas P. Jahnige, *The Federal Courts as a Political System* (New York: Harper & Row, 1971), p. 148.

63. Herbert Jacob, *Justice in America*, 2d ed. (Boston: Little, Brown & Co., 1972), p. 221.

64. Goldman and Jahnige, pp. 248–49. See also David W. Rohde and Harold J. Spaeth, *Supreme Court Decision Making* (San Francisco: W. H. Freeman & Co., 1976), p. 66. Note that these writers were all considering federal courts where judges are appointed for life. One might reasonably infer that the impact of public opinion might be greater on judges who are elected, but see the discussion in the text on pp. 25–26.

65. Grey thesis, p. 173.

66. Ibid., p. 220. Rohde and Spaeth note that the chief justice is conscious of public relations in his selection of opinion writers. Rohde and Spaeth, p. 176. And the anecdotal evidence provided by Woodward and Armstrong suggests strongly that this is also characteristic of some associate justices. See generally Bob Woodward and Scott Armstrong, *The Brethren* (New York: Simon and Schuster, 1979).

67. Stanga, p. 166.

68. Ibid., p. 167.

69. James Eisenstein, *Politics and the Legal Process* (New York: Harper & Row, 1973), p. 109.

70. Ibid., p. 104. It may well be, however, that prosecutors must be highly attuned to public opinion since the reputations they build in political circles could be crucial to, say, their ultimate accession to the bench. Also, the nature of their work—their constant focus on criminal offenders—is something in which the public has an obvious, constant and quite direct interest.

71. Jacob, p. 139. See also James Eisenstein and Herbert Jacob, *Felony Justice: An Organizational Analysis of Criminal Courts* (Boston: Little, Brown & Co., 1977), pp. 57–58, 93–94, 122–23, 166–67. That the press reports only a small minority of cases is worth emphasizing. One study has found that in a Midwestern city of 100,000, only 39 of 234 criminal charges were reported. Thomas E. Eimermann and Rita James Simon, "Newspaper Coverage of Crimes and Trials: Another Empirical Look at the Free Press–Fair Trial Controversy," *Journalism Quarterly* 47 (1970):142–43. Another study found that during one month nearly 20 percent of 80 community newspapers in Minnesota reported no local court news at all. Robert Drechsel, Kermit Netteburg and Bisi Aborisade, "Community Size and Newspaper Reporting of Local Courts," *Journalism Quarterly* 57 (Spring 1980):74.

72. Seth A. Goldschlager, "The Law and the News Media" (Thesis, Yale Law

School, 1971), pp. 42–44, cited by Everette E. Dennis, "Another Look at Press Coverage of the Supreme Court," *Villanova Law Review* 20 (1974–75):779.

73. Ibid.

74. *Minnesota Clerk's Manual*, p. 1. The role of the court clerk may be quite significant. One study of state court clerks concluded that their power has been greatly underestimated and noted that they almost totally control all information for local courts. Larry Berkson and Steven Hays, "The Forgotten Politicians: Court Clerks," *University of Miami Law Review* 30 (Spring 1976):499–516.

75. For example, note how several U.S. Supreme Court justices negatively responded to an overt attempt at lobbying. See Woodward and Armstrong, pp. 79–85.

76. I do not mean to suggest that the nature of legislative or executive decision making and judicial decision making are mutually exclusive. Certainly the nonjudicial branches gather their own information too; and undoubtedly some of the information on which the judicial branch acts may be produced by the news media. The difference is one of degree.

77. Grey thesis, p. 211. Of course, the judicial system may have internal communication problems of its own. See, e.g., S. Sidney Ulmer, "The Supreme Court Opinion as a Communications Device," paper presented at the 1980 annual meeting of the American Political Science Association, Washington, D.C., 28–31 August 1980.

78. Larry Charles Berkson, *The Supreme Court and Its Publics* (Lexington, Mass.: Lexington Books, 1978), pp. 63–64. The other specialized publics included doctors, clergy members, school teachers, bookstore operators, movie theatre operators, school board members and lawmakers.

79. Richard M. Johnson, *The Dynamics of Compliance* (Evanston, Ill.: Northwestern University Press, 1967), p. 95.

80. Anthony Lewis, "Problems of a Washington Correspondent," *Connecticut Bar Journal* 33 (1959):36.

81. See, for example, Grey thesis, p. 211. See also Lewis, p. 363. For an indication of how different the situation is in other areas of government, see Hess, pp. 55–63, 99–100. For example, Hess found that one major reason journalists preferred to gather information from the legislative branch was the willingness of legislators and aides to talk. Hess, p. 99.

82. Chester A. Newland, "Press Coverage of the United States Supreme Court," *Western Political Quarterly* 17 (March 1964):16. This observation is confirmed by Hess, who found that logs kept for him by five Supreme Court reporters during an "unusually busy" week showed strikingly little use of interviews. Hess, p. 58.

83. Grey thesis, pp. 248–49.

84. Grey thesis, pp. 177–78.

85. F. Dennis Hale, "The Court's Perception of the Press," *Judicature* 57 (December 1973):186–87.

86. F. Dennis Hale, "How Reporters and Justices View Coverage of a State Appellate Court," *Journalism Quarterly* 52 (Spring 1975):109.

87. Robert E. Drechsel, "How Minnesota Newspapers Cover the Trial Courts," *Judicature* 62 (October 1978):199.

88. Berg, p. 14.

89. Ibid., p. 16.

90. Deborah Unitus Bereznak, "Public Information Needs Concerning Maryland's Courts—an Assessment" (Annapolis, Md.: Administrative Office of the State Courts, 1979), p. 29.

91. *Minnesota Clerk's Manual*, p. 14.

92. *News Media and D.C. Courts*, pp. 7, 14–16.

93. Eisenstein, pp. 48–49.

94. Ibid., p. 33. Eisenstein cites the example of Louisiana, where 90 percent of the state's elected judges who are on the bench at age 45 remain there until retirement. Jacob cites the example of Minnesota where one study found that elected state district court judges held office longer than life-term federal judges. Jacob, p. 109.

95. For example, a study of supreme court justices in Minnesota found that of the justices who served between 1858 and 1968, 87 percent had held other government offices but only 52 percent had prior judicial experience. See Robert A. Heiberg, "Social Backgrounds of the Minnesota Supreme Court Justices: 1858–1968," *Minnesota Law Review* 53 (April 1969):924–27.

96. Richardson and Vines have concluded that there is little hierarchical movement in the federal court system, and that "the lack of lower federal court experience for 80 percent of the Supreme Court justices makes 'judicial promotion' of less significance than we might have assumed." Richard J. Richardson and Kenneth N. Vines, *"The Politics of Federal Courts: Lower Courts in the United States* (Boston: Little, Brown & Co., 1970), pp. 160–61. See also Joel B. Grossman, *Lawyers and Judges: The ABA and the Politics of Judicial Selection* (New York: John Wiley & Sons, 1965), p. 204. Heiberg's Minnesota study found that the percentage of state supreme court justices with prior judicial experience has actually been decreasing since 1931. Heiberg, p. 927.

97. All federal judges are appointed for life. Although state judges are generally elected, many states initially appoint judges and voters subsequently decide only whether "Judge X" shall be retained. Even in states where judges are subject to competitive elections, judges frequently are first appointed to the bench. For example, see Albert P. Melone, "Political Realities and Democratic Ideals: Accession and Competition in a State Judicial System," *North Dakota Law Review* 54 (1977):187–208.

98. Grossman, p. 42.

99. Sheldon Goldman, "Judicial Appointments to the United States Courts of Appeals," *Wisconsin Law Review* 1967:213–14.

100. Ibid., pp. 208–10. Of course, media coverage might bring a judge's name to officials' attention initially, but there is no evidence of this.

101. For illustrations of the degree of voter ignorance in judicial elections, see Charles A. Johnson, Roger C. Shaefer and R. Neal McKnight, "The Salience of Judicial Candidates and Elections," *Social Science Quarterly* 59 (September 1978):376; and David Adamany and Philip Dubois, "Electing State Judges," *Wisconsin Law Review* 1976:775.

102. Eisenstein, p. 69. For specific support for this generalization, see William Jenkins, Jr., "Retention Elections: Who Wins When No One Loses," *Judicature* 61 (August 1977):80; Malcolm C. Moos, "Judicial Elections and Partisan Endorsements of Judicial Candidates in Minnesota," *American Political Science Review* 35 (1941):69; Heiberg, pp. 903–904; and Eisenstein, p. 29.

103. A study in North Dakota found that 80 percent of the state's district court

judges were initially appointed and that 87 percent of them were unopposed in their first primary election bid—a number especially striking since North Dakota judicial elections are nonpartisan. Melone, pp. 194, 198. See also Herbert Jacob, "Judicial Insulation—Elections, Direct Participation and Public Attention to the Courts in Wisconsin," *Wisconsin Law Review* 1966:806.

104. Jacob, "Judicial Insulation," p. 819.

105. Eisenstein, p. 31; Moos, p. 72; Adamany and Dubois, p. 778. See also Philip L. Dubois, "The Significance of Voting Cues in State Supreme Court Elections," *Law and Society Review* 13 (Spring 1979):757–79. Adamany and Dubois (p. 776) note that if judges are relatively unaccountable to the electorate in partisan elections, they are even more unaccountable in nonpartisan elections. Minnesota's judicial elections are nonpartisan.

106. Jacob, "Judicial Insulation," p. 819.

107. Eisenstein, p. 27.

108. Ibid., pp. 20–25. And not surprisingly, Eisenstein (p. 27) notes that elections can operate as a direct control on prosecutors more than on judges.

3

A Historical Review of Newspaper Court Reporting

The history of published reports of judicial action is little younger than the history of printing itself. Published news of local courts can be traced at least to the sixteenth century. Before—and even during—the age of the newspaper, numerous ballads, broadsheets, newsletters, pamphlets and books chronicled sensational criminal cases and trials. For example, a Fugger newsletter, in 1587, gave a detailed account of a witchcraft trial. It began with this approximation of a summary lead:

> Walpurga Hausmannin, evil and wretched woman, now imprisoned and in chains has, under solicitous questioning as well as torture, confessed her witchcraft and made the following admissions.[1]

According to Matthias Shaaber, after 1575, "it hardly seems possible that a really first-rate murder, especially if it was complicated by an illicit love affair, or the hanging of any notable criminal went unrecorded, while the very best of them . . . inspired numerous effusions of the popular press [mostly ballads]."[2]

Shaaber believes that most reports of judicial proceedings, at least in the early 1600s, were composed by the courts' own secretaries and clerks because officials generally wouldn't permit verbatim publication of their records except under their own supervision.[3] Nevertheless, others did some publishing, notably clergymen who attended condemned criminals.[4]

By the mid-seventeenth century, some newspapers were printing accounts of court cases—primarily criminal cases. The format was generally a terse, one- or two-line account. For example, a newspaper in 1656 noted the following case:

> David Old, and Agnes Dick his Wives brothers daughter for Incest with other, confest judicially, and found guilty thereof by an Assise, ordained on the first Wednesday of June next to the ordinary place of execution for the Burgh of Air, and there betwixt two and four hours in the afternoon, to be hanged till they be dead, and all their movable Goods to be Escheat.[5]

Sometimes, however, the account could run to some length. Joseph Frank notes that one English editor in the 1640s filled two pages with a report from a London murder trial.[6] The same editor later published such stories as accounts of the trial of a woman with fifteen husbands and a jury casting lots to decide the fate of a defendant in a rape case.[7]

By the early eighteenth century, there was sufficient coverage of courts to lead one newspaper editor to complain that

> the proceedings of our Courts, in the Tryal of Rapes, Criminal Conversations, and something still more abominable, at which Trials, whenever they came on, the late Lord Chief Justice Holt would often give notice to his Female Auditors are now printed in Words at length, or with such Marks and Breaks as are easily intelligible. The Proceedings in Doctors Commons upon Cases of Divorce, have been carefully translated from the Latin, in which, according to the Rules of the Court, they are decently conceal'd.[8]

The main vehicle for court reporting in the eighteenth century was not, however, the newspaper. It was the specialized crime publication— either as broadside, pamphlet or book. Newspapers tended to be too small (two to four pages) for complete coverage, and those pages often favored essays over news. The specialized publications, on the other hand, offered verbatim reports of trials, often embellished with description, or sometimes narrative reports.[9] Peterson, who studied these publications, concluded that most pamphlet and book publishers did their work "at least fairly well"—that is, with substantial accuracy and a minimum of lurid content. Broadside publishers, however, "typified the yellow press."[10]

But it was the beginning of the nineteenth century before newspapers moved into the market aggressively. In the early 1820s, the *London Morning Herald* had employed John Wight as police court reporter, and his work was so popular that it was quickly collected into book form.[11] His style was the humorous narrative, taking some liberty with the facts and often making fun of the defendants. Such behavior led a contemporary to complain that

> the penny and two-penny unstamped and illegal papers . . . had outgrown the intentions of those who at first favoured them, and Frankensteinlike, were become objects of horror to those who at first played with them—they had slipped the bridle and were . . . trampling under foot every consideration of decency or morality, and threatening annihilation to every principle of sound politics and true religion.[12]

Clearly Wight was aware of such criticism. He justified his reporting as a means by which "the prosperous and orderly portion of society can know what passes among the destitute and disorderly portion of it; that they can rightly appreciate the advantages they enjoy, and the value and importance of these particular institutions of their country."[13]

American local court reporting apparently began much as it did in England—with the pamphlet. Shaaber, who has also studied forerunners of the American newspaper, notes that little news of any kind was published in the colonies before 1665, and there was no private commercial printing until 1675.[14] But in 1692, William Bradford published a pamphlet chronicling a murder trial in transcript form.[15] Apparently this medium continued to be used for some time; a 1729 issue of the *Boston News-Letter* carried an advertisement announcing forthcoming publication of two crime/trial pamphlets, one of which carried the hefty title of:

> The Trials of Five Persons for Piracy, Felony and Robbery, Who were found Guilty and Condemned, at a Court of Admiralty, Held in Boston NE on Tuesday the 4th day of October, 1726, and Executed, Nov. 2 following.[16]

But what of the American newspapers? They are the topic of the remainder of this chapter.

One of the gaps in the scholarly study of the history of journalism has been in the history of news gathering itself.[17] If this is generally true, it is specifically true for the history of newspaper court reporting. This lack of historical context is particularly surprising in light of the perennial discussion of fair trial versus free press and general criticism of the competence of court reporting.

This chapter, then, provides some missing historical context by tracing the beginnings and development of newspaper court reporting in the United States. More specifically, this chapter addresses such questions as who reporters were, what they covered, how they did their jobs, what sources they used, how they reported the information they gathered, how the answers to these questions changed over time and what factors may have affected these historical developments.

METHOD

This study examines American court reporting from 1704 to the turn of the twentieth century. It is limited to reporting on courts of original jurisdiction; reporting on appellate courts was not studied. Only locally written stories about local courts were considered. And only news stories—not editorials—were included. Within those bounds, secondary and primary sources were consulted. Journalism histories, biographies, newspaper histories, journal articles and even some early reporting textbooks were searched for material relevant to court reporting. Relatively little was found; consequently, the primary sources are the foundation of the study.

Major journalism histories were used to select a representative sample of the American press beginning in 1704.[18] Some attempt was made at geographic representativeness, but newspapers were selected primarily according to how well they represented their time period, because of their role in journalistic innovation and/or because of their temporal continuity.

The newspapers, the time frame of the sample and the frequency of publication included: *The Boston News-Letter* (1704–1776, weekly); *Boston Gazette* (1719–1798, weekly); *Boston Evening Post* (1735–1775, weekly); *Boston Transcript* (1830–1900, daily); Bradford's *New York Gazette* (1726–1744, weekly); *New York Evening Post* (1801–1902, daily); *New York Herald* (1835–1895, daily); *New York Tribune* (1841–1902, daily); *Pennsylvania Gazette* (1728–1815, weekly); *Philadelphia Aurora* (1790–1814, daily); *Philadelphia Public Ledger* (1836–1897, daily); *Chicago Tribune* (1847–1895, daily).[19]

I attempted to at least scan, at five-year intervals, almost every issue of the weekly newspapers for local court coverage, and this was possible because the newspapers were very small (generally four small pages) and predictably organized.[20] But a more sophisticated method of sampling became necessary for the daily newspapers, particularly beginning with the *New York Herald* and the *New York Tribune*. Therefore, the dailies were sampled by using a random-numbers table to select 25 issues of each paper at 10-year intervals.

Figure 3.1 illustrates how the sampled newspapers cover the total time frame. At first glance, the scope of this study seems unmanageable. Indeed, it is true that one reason the project ended with the turn of the century was the practical, logistic difficulty of handling more and larger newspapers. Nevertheless, scope presented relatively little difficulty. For all of the eighteenth century and for at least the first two decades of the nineteenth, newspapers remained small and quite compartmentalized. Scanning and reading proved to be somewhat time-consuming but not un-

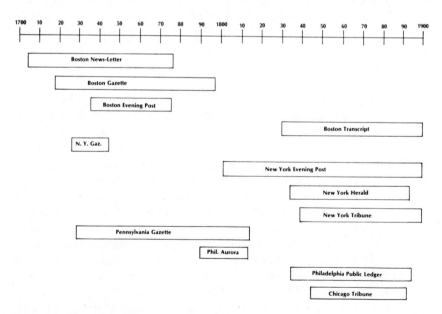

Figure 3.1 Time Line of Newspapers Sampled

reasonably difficult. Even after the 1830s, newspapers were not the bulky multisection products they have become today. Again, the relatively small size, coupled with the news being generally compartmentalized, made sampling and reading manageable chores. The work became particularly time-consuming and difficult only near the end of the nineteenth century. One other factor contributed to the manageability of the scope: lack of change. That is, so little change was detected in content over the bulk of the period that sampling at 10-year intervals was clearly justified. In fact, 15- or 20-year intervals may have worked just as well.

Before turning to the findings of this study, we must consider two preliminary questions: What was the nature of the early American judicial system that newspapers covered? and How open to the press was that system?

JUDICIAL STRUCTURE AND ACCESSIBILITY

The English judicial system was not quickly, directly and entirely transplanted to the colonies. Many colonists deeply distrusted lawyers, and such feelings lasted into the eighteenth century. In fact, several colonies went so far as to exclude lawyers from their courts.[21] Besides, colonial society was hardly as complex as that on the other side of the Atlantic, and it did not demand a complex judicial structure. The Plymouth colony survived for years without any provision for officials to act specifically as judges.[22] In Massachusetts Bay, the first inferior courts were established in 1639, but until then, the governor and assistants handled all cases.[23] Nor was it unusual for early courts to have some quasi-legislative and executive power besides judicial power.[24] Francis H. Heller, a scholar of the Sixth Amendment, believes the jury trial guarantee of that amendment is relatively vague at least partially because the American concept of jury trial

> reflects the fact that there was at first a period of rude, untechnical popular law, an attempt by laymen to order their affairs by themselves in an atmosphere of profound hostility toward the legal profession and their methods.[25]

By the beginning of the eighteenth century, however, the need for the much despised lawyer was becoming apparent and colonial judicial systems began taking a form still recognizable. Massachusetts, Pennsylvania and New York—the colonies whose newspapers are the subject of this study—developed roughly similar judicial systems. At the base was a magistrate or justice of the peace before whom those accused of offenses would appear for preliminary inquiry (or for disposition of the case if it was quite trivial). At least in serious criminal cases, this official would decide whether to hold a person for trial. Several times a year, a court of original jurisdiction would convene to try such persons.[26] Civil cases were often handled by separate courts.[27]

In their study of law enforcement in colonial New York, Julius Goebel and T. Raymond Naughton describe a typical serious criminal case: the victim appeared before a magistrate and entered an accusation by affidavit or oath; the accused was brought by a constable or sheriff to the magistrate and examined; if he found sufficient cause, the magistrate would order the accused to appear at the next sessions of the peace, oyer and terminer or supreme court session (these were courts of original jurisdiction); there a grand jury would hear the evidence and decide whether to indict; if there was an indictment, trial would follow.[28]

There was apparently little concept of due process as we know it today. According to Goebel and Naughton, trials were usually one-sided, since the crown would be represented by a competent attorney general, while the defendant seldom had counsel and had to rely on the good offices of the judges for advice.[29]

As cities—particularly Boston, New York and Philadelphia—grew, so did caseloads. As the nineteenth century began, courts began to be in session almost continuously. Meanwhile, of course, a federal court system had been added.

There is no reason to doubt that court proceedings and records were open to the public. The Massachusetts Body of Liberties of 1641 provided for both open courts and open records:

> Sec. 76—Whensoever any Jurie of trialls or jourours are not cleare in their judgements or consciences. . . . They shall have libertie in open Court to advise with any man . . . before they give in their verdict.

> Sec. 48—Every Inhabitant of the Country shall have free libertie to search and veewe any Rooles, Records, or Regesters of any Court or office except the Councell, and to have a transcript or exemplification thereof written, examined and signed by the hand of the officer of the office paying the appointed fees therefore.[30]

Pennsylvania's 1682 frame of government specified that courts shall be open.[31] The 1677 Concessions and Agreements of West Jersey were even more explicit:

> . . . in all publick courts of justice for tryals of causes, civil or criminal, any person or persons, inhabitants of the said Province may freely come into, and attend the said courts, and hear and be present, at all or any such tryals as shall be there had or passed, that justice may not be done in a corner nor in any covert manner. . . .[32]

After declaring independence, Pennsylvania, Delaware, North Carolina and Vermont put public trial provisions in their new constitutions.[33] And, of course, the Sixth Amendment of the U.S. Constitution granted criminal defendants in federal cases the right to a public trial.

Apparently, preliminary hearings in criminal cases were also routinely open and could be fully reported.[34]

In sum, there is no reason to believe that the colonial or early republican press had serious difficulty obtaining access to judicial proceedings or documents. With this very basic knowledge of the judicial system, we can return to a discussion of court reporting.

FINDINGS

The findings are divided into six basic categories: evidence on who the reporters were; what the press covered; how reporters did their jobs; what sources reporters used; bias, color and style in reporting; and criticism. The discussion section, which follows, considers factors which may have influenced court reporting and relates historical evidence to this study's research questions.

Who Were the Early Reporters?

There is no doubt that American newspapers were covering local courts early in the eighteenth century. But who was doing the reporting? Unfortunately, it is nearly impossible to know—at least beyond the generalization that the editor was generally his own reporter and that local news was "such as could be obtained from official or semi-official sources or could easily be picked up by the printer-editor."[35] Kobre notes that John Campbell, publisher of the *Boston News-Letter*, obtained his news without a paid reporter.[36] And Mott states that even the largest newspapers generally had no reporters for local items until the 1840s.[37] He believes that until at least 1833 the majority of editors were still printers and that "even on the largest papers, the editor was commonly his own reporter. ... With the prevailing disregard for local news, reporting had as yet no standing."[38] This squares with A. M. Lee's conclusion that even during the late 1820s, the daily newspaper editorial staff consisted of two or three political writers and one news editor who was also a general reporter.[39]

The 1820s provide the first concrete evidence about reporters, although even that evidence is sketchy. We know, for example, that James Gordon Bennett in the late 1820s wrote a verbatim report of a bank fraud case for the *National Advocate*[40] and that he was apparently reporting on major trials involving insurance company scandals in 1826.[41] He also covered a celebrated murder case in Massachusetts for the *New York Courier and Enquirer* in 1830,[42] and has been called the "first real reporter the American Press [has] known."[43] When Bennett became a publisher, he hired a police reporter in 1835,[44] although Bleyer credits the *Morning Courier* and one or two other New York papers with the first police court reporting in 1828.[45]

Obtaining insight into these early reporters more specifically and individually is difficult. The primary sources are of little assistance, other than as evidence that early reporters were highly literate, possibly possessed of some technical knowledge of the law and apparently proficient at shorthand.

For example, Thomas Gill, court reporter for the *Boston Morning Post*, was able occasionally to discuss precedent in his humorous police court stories. On one occasion, after citing an English precedent, he explained:

> As our chief aim in our reports of judicial proceedings, is only to instruct the present generation in the weighty matters of the law, we sometimes undertake to accomplish our laudable design, by going back to former decisions, and citing them in application to recent cases, that the beauty thereof may be manifest to the reader.[46]

A much later example may be seen in a *New York Evening Post* story on a civil case involving an explosion. The reporter wrote that

> in most of the cases where the insurers have been held liable for the havoc wrought by an explosion, the explosion has occurred within the structure damaged. Whether the courts will so construe the explosion clause as to include liability for damage done by explosions at distant points is the question of chief interest.[47]

Of course, it is impossible to know how such reporters came by their legal knowledge. One possibility is that they actually used legal reference materials; but another is that they were briefed by attorneys or other experts. A hint comes from the *Post's* advertisement for a court reporter:

> Wanted—A competent person to assist as a legal reporter for the Evening Post. None need apply who have not been bred to the legal profession. Gentlemen will please transmit their address and references, in writing, to our office of publication. . . .[48]

Unfortunately, we cannot know precisely what the *Post* meant by "bred to the legal profession." Yet by the 1880s there is evidence that at least some court reporters were college-educated. A reporter for the *Chicago Tribune* in 1885 reported the following exchange with a man being held for trial on kidnaping charges:

> "Say," said he eying the Tribune reporter through the bars, "I know you."
> "Yes, you met me at the university in 1882."
> "Yes, yes! the year I graduated . . ."[49]

Perhaps this is also suggestive of reporters' ages, although such a generalization would be risky. Nevertheless, one reasonable inference would be that even by the mid-nineteenth century, newspaper court reporters were no longer a cadre of Englishmen hired to imitate the successful *London Morning Herald's* police court reporters.[50] Perhaps, too, the typical reporter was no longer a person "graduated" from being a printer in a type foundry.[51]

What Did Newspapers Cover?

Journalism historians have tended to agree that until the third or fourth decades of the nineteenth century, American newspapers provided little local news. Mott concluded that eighteenth-century newspapers were "very neglectful" of local news, although "we must remember that towns were so small that everyone knew what was going on."[52] Bleyer found only "a little" local news in colonial newspapers.[53] A. M. Lee concluded that early American daily newspapers also paid little heed to local events and that until well into the nineteenth century most of their content "was gleaned from coffee-house books and newspapers or from their own exchanges."[54] Mott agrees, observing that

> [from 1801 to 1833] local or home news, which would have been easy to obtain, remained largely an untilled field. . . . Papers in the smaller places usually printed the deaths and marriages, gave a few lines to a bad fire or storm, and "played" at a greater length any political meetings or important crime events that might occur. But such home events were meagrely treated in the weeklies, and the larger dailies were little better in this respect.[55]

Until recently, there has been little reason to doubt that the same generalizations applied to court news. For example, Mott noted that eighteenth-century American newspapers did give "many paragraphs" to piracy, privateering, fires, counterfeiting, murders, robberies and suicides, but he does not specifically mention court news.[56] The generally accepted interpretation has been that court news was primarily a discovery of the penny press. Schudson, in a social history of American journalism, concludes that the penny press marked the first instance of newspapers printing court reports.[57] Lee found that until well into the nineteenth century, daily newspapers restricted court news to reports on trials involving commercial or political matters and to brief coverage of some murders.[58] Bleyer concluded that no American newspaper published police court stories regularly until they became leading features in the first penny papers.[59]

Bleyer's statement is probably the most accurate. But there are exceptions to Lee's unqualified conclusion and as the following analysis of primary data shows, Schudson has greatly overstated the case.[60]

Criminal cases.   From the first part of the eighteenth century, American newspapers covered all aspects of the criminal process—preliminary examinations, inquests, grand jury proceedings, trials and sentencings. Even some of the earliest coverage was remarkably detailed. For example, in 1719 the *Boston News-Letter* covered the preliminary examination of a man charged with counterfeiting:

> . . . upon examination [he] owned, that whilst he was in London (from whence he lately arrived in the Ship Providence) he met one Briant in George Yard on Tower Hill an engraver by Trade, who told him if he was a

New-England Man, he had a Commodity that would suit him well, shewing him a Twenty Shilling Massachusetts Bill of Credit, and. . . . [61]

The story proceeds with similar detail.

In 1727, the *New York Gazette* gave detailed coverage, including a full column of verbatim testimony, to a preliminary examination in a counterfeiting case.[62] The *Gazette* also provides an early example of grand jury coverage. A story in 1734 reported a grand jury presentment against two scandalous, malicious songs defamatory of the colonial administration and included a verbatim report of a court order requiring the offending material to be burned in front of the city hall.[63]

Coverage of trials was generally brief, but can be traced to some of the earliest newspapers. An example from the *Boston Gazette* is representative:

Last Week at the Superiour Court of Judicature, Joseph, a Negro Man, was Tryed, and found Guilty of Barbarously Murdering his Wife, and accordingly received Sentence of Death.[64]

There is even reason to believe that early in the eighteenth century, at least some newspapers were covering most of the serious criminal cases tried in their communities. Stories compiling the results of such cases frequently appeared during court terms. These compilations generally consisted of the name of the defendant, the specific charge, perhaps some characterization of the evidence presented, and the disposition.[65] Nor was it unusual for colonial newspapers to provide continuing coverage as a case developed. An example from the *Boston News-Letter* is typical (and incidentally demonstrates that early newspapers were not reluctant to cover distasteful cases). In May 1733, the paper reported that

on Friday last a young Woman of this Town, named Rebecca Chamblet was committed to Goal, being charged by the Coroner's Inquest, with the Murder of her Spurious Male Infant; which by her confession she was deliver'd of alone the Tuesday before, in a little House; and, as she said, finding it to be dead, threw it down the Vault, hoping thereby to conceal it, and where, after diligent Search, the poor Babe was found.[66]

Three months later, the *News-Letter* reported that

Tuesday last in the Forenoon, at the Superiour Court holden here for the County of Suffolk, came on the tryal of Rebecca Chamblet. . . . It being committed to the jury, in the Afternoon they brought her in Guilty.[67]

And the following week, we are told that

Rebecca Chamblet received Sentence of Death last Thursday for the Murder of her Bastard Child, and the 27th Day of Next Month is appointed for her execution.[68]

As already noted, coverage was occasionally more detailed, but in general form it remained substantially unchanged until at least the 1820s.

Most important is the conclusion that coverage of criminal cases did in fact appear in American newspapers from the earliest days, that these newspapers apparently did not consider any type of criminal court action too distasteful to cover, and that the evolution of criminal court coverage during the eighteenth and nineteenth centuries may have been more one of degree than kind.[69]

Civil cases.   Examples of stories on civil actions can be found at least as far back as 1738 when the *Boston Evening Post* reported that

> Last Thursday there was another trial at the Superiour Court now holden here, between the Town of Boston and the Heirs of James Everill, upon Review, for Part of the Interest on the Town Dock: The Trial lasted from Eleven O'Clock in the Forenoon till near Four the next Morning, when it was committed to the Jury, who in the Afternoon brought in their Verdict in favour of the Town.[70]

But coverage of civil cases was rare until well into the nineteenth century. Yet only a year after its founding in 1841, the *New York Tribune* was reporting a great deal of civil court action ranging from bad debt cases to probate actions. Early in the 1850s, civil coverage seems to have equaled or exceeded criminal coverage in the *New York Evening Post*. Salvage, foreclosure and probate cases received considerable attention. By 1872, the *Tribune* had standing headlines for civil actions, and an occasional civil suit received front-page attention.[71]

In summary, although civil cases were generally ignored throughout the eighteenth century, they received a great deal of coverage from the press beginning in the mid-nineteenth century.[72] This conclusion holds generally for all the newspapers considered in this study.

Miscellaneous coverage.   Judicial coverage in the eighteenth and nineteenth centuries was not confined to coverage of cases. As early as 1737, for example, the *Boston Gazette* reported on an attorney's admission to the bar.[73] And in 1741, the same newspaper reported on the removal from office of two justices of the peace "for encouraging the Notes commonly called the Manufactory Bills, and persisting therein."[74] In 1772, the *Boston Evening Post* reported the salaries of the justices of superior court, the attorney general and the solicitor general.[75]

In the nineteenth century, coverage of the judicial system itself (as opposed to coverage of cases) increased. Clearly, such coverage was nowhere near as common as coverage of cases, but it did exist.

For one thing, newspapers began to pay more attention to the bar. Already in 1846, the *New York Herald* published a report on a city bar association meeting, although the coverage appeared to be a reprint of minutes of the meeting.[76] In 1862, the *New York Evening Post* reported on an investigation of a man's admission to the New York bar, noting that "the whole subject has created the liveliest interest among the profession, and is a fruitful topic of gossip around the courts and in the law offices."[77]

During the 1870s, coverage of the bar appeared in the *Post*, the *Herald* and the *Chicago Tribune*.[78] In fact, in 1875, an issue of the *Chicago Tribune* devoted five full columns to a nearly verbatim report of proceedings at an annual banquet of the Chicago Bar Association.[79] Bar association coverage appeared in the *Philadelphia Public Ledger* in the 1880s.[80]

Judges, too, received some press attention. Already in 1842, the *New York Tribune* reported on a meeting of local judges.[81] And in 1887, the *Philadelphia Public Ledger* published a story on court of common pleas action modifying a new court rule.[82] Generally, however, judges received notably less coverage than attorneys.

What may have been the first critical reporting on the judicial branch appeared as early as 1862 when the *New York Tribune* published a short piece critical of the conduct of a police justice.[83] Ten years later, the same paper undertook some full-fledged investigative reporting on the ease with which a person could be committed to an institution for lunacy.[84] In the early 1870s, the *New York Evening Post* publicized a report from a group called the Council of Political Reform that suggested corruption and incompetence problems among police court justices.[85] Meanwhile, the *Chicago Tribune* exposed allegedly exorbitant fees charged by justices of the peace and constables.[86] And the *New York Herald* publicized a comptroller's investigation into fee charges and bookkeeping by court clerks.[87]

One other genre of story that surfaced in the nineteenth century was the analysis story. Evidence of such a type occurs, for example, in the *Chicago Tribune* in 1875 when a reporter gathered a considerable range of official reaction to and speculation about a judge's ruling against the city's method of collecting delinquent taxes.[88] Such stories were unusual.

In sum, the judicial system in the mid- to late 1800s began to receive some scrutiny beyond spot news coverage of cases. But such enterprising coverage was rare, accounting for only a miniscule portion of all court coverage.

Courts covered. One final indicator of what early reporters covered is the number of courts that received attention. Table 3.1 lists the courts that newspapers in this study covered. To appear on the list, a court must have received attention more than once. In fact, the newspapers covered these courts quite frequently, if not exhaustively.[89]

How Did Reporters Do Their Jobs?

Finding evidence about the nature of the reporting process in the eighteenth century is difficult. Some useful insight is provided by consideration of the sources newspapers used, but sources will be the topic of the next section. There is reason to believe, however, that journalists were observing court firsthand quite early.

TABLE 3.1   Courts Covered by Eighteenth- and Nineteenth-Century Newspapers

Newspapers	Courts
Boston News-Letter, *Gazette* and *Evening Post*	Superior Justice of the peace Admiralty Common pleas General sessions of the peace
New York Gazette	Mayor and magistrates Supreme Oyer and terminer
Philadelphia Aurora	Mayor's court U.S. circuit court
Boston Transcript	Municipal Superior U.S. circuit
New York Evening Post, *Herald* and *Tribune*	Supreme Superior Common pleas Police Chancery Oyer and terminer Surrogate General sessions Marine U.S. district
Philadelphia Public Ledger	Police Mayor's Quarter sessions Oyer and terminer Recorders Supreme Orphans Common pleas U.S. district U.S. commissioner
Chicago Tribune	Recorders Common pleas U.S. district Police Circuit Superior County Probate

NOTE: All the courts are primarily courts of original jurisdiction. Some handled criminal matters (e.g., general sessions, oyer and terminer and police court); others handled civil cases (e.g., common pleas); and others were courts of more general jurisdiction (e.g., superior court).

For example, in 1734, the *Boston News-Letter* went beyond mere reporting of the facts of a case and noted that when two men received death sentences for murder and burglary, "Ormseby said little or nothing: But Cushing behav'd himself in a very unbecoming manner, speaking with much Levity and great Confidence, both during his Trial, and at the Time when he had his Sentence."[90] In a story two years later, the *News-Letter* reported that a man accused of kidnaping "publickly own'd this Vile attempt and boldly justify'd himself in it."[91]

There are fairly numerous examples of colonial newspapers presenting testimony—sometimes verbatim—from preliminary examinations and trials,[92] but it is impossible to know whether the journalists were using court records, clerks' or judges' memories, other sources or their own firsthand observation to obtain the information. For example, in 1773, the *Boston Evening Post* reported the acquittal of a man charged with piracy and robbery on the high seas. The story directly quoted some of the accused man's remarks to the court, noting that he "respectfully bowed to the Court, and said,—'I thank the honorable Court—and God—for my Deliverance!'"[93] Occasionally, a story would characterize a court proceeding in a way suggesting the presence of a reporter. For example, the *New York Evening Post* noted in its extensive coverage of a show-cause hearing in 1807 that "much time was consumed and a great deal of learning displayed in the endeavor to establish a proposition which nobody disputes."[94]

Much less guesswork is necessary after 1820. Perhaps the best overall description of the development of news gathering is provided by A. M. Lee. According to Lee, early news beats were not extensive. In Philadelphia, for example, even after the founding of the *Public Ledger* in 1836, reporters were not considered essential to a newspaper's success but were considered hunters for "unconsidered trifles."[95] Until the 1850s, newspapers in Philadelphia divided the city geographically for news gathering and shared information.[96] As late as 1840, the chief editor of a New York newspaper rarely had more than two or three assistants.[97]

But some of the first men hired as reporters were court reporters. James Gordon Bennett was covering court cases as early as the mid-1820s.[98] And a historian of the *Boston Transcript* credits that newspaper's successful beginning to coverage of a murder case.[99] There is evidence that the *New York Evening Post* employed a court reporter as early as 1827 because a byline occasionally credited stories as "reported for the New York Evening Post."[100] The *Boston Transcript* had such a reporter by 1831.[101] And we know that Ben Day wasted no time hiring George Wisner as police court reporter at $4 per week plus a share of the profits.[102]

The more fundamental question is how did these reporters go about doing their jobs? Evidence presented by Bleyer indicates that in the mid-1830s, the *New York Evening Transcript* and the *New York Sun* had police court reporters spending from 3 A.M. to 8 P.M. daily in court.[103] Parton tells us that by 1855, the *New York Tribune* had a law reporter and a police court reporter.[104] Presumably, the law reporter covered all courts aside from police court. He also tells us that reporters checked in early in the afternoon but returned to do their writing in the evening.[105] According to Lee, by 1870, the *New York Herald* and *New York Times* had as many as twenty-three local reporters each, and metropolitan dailies had developed staff organizations much like those today.[106]

A reading of the primary sources leads to two major conclusions about the development of the court-reporting process during the nineteenth century: reporters began to use more and more sources; and reporters began to make heavy use of the interview in conjunction with documents and direct observation of proceedings. This more active role began to supplement the traditional near-verbatim reporting of proceedings, although even at the end of the nineteenth century some verbatim reporting survived.

For example, the *Chicago Tribune* in 1875 gave extensive coverage to an inquest after an apparent murder. The first one and a half columns of the story were confined to substantially verbatim reporting of the testimony. But another full column was devoted to a verbatim account of a *Tribune* reporter's interview with the suspect. The reporter also wrote that he called on the state's attorney to inquire how soon the incident would go to a grand jury. He then quoted unnamed sources as agreeing that the suspect should be hung and apparently visited several "gambling haunts" to observe the reaction there.[107]

In 1882, a *New York Evening Post* reporter began by talking with a defendant in police court, went to the man's mother to corroborate his story and then visited the mother's neighbor to corroborate her story.[108] And a *New York Herald* story in 1886 on a bribery trial clearly indicates that a reporter talked to the defendant, a "visiting lawyer," an ex-assemblyman, a "22nd district politician," a "well known official who would not consent to have his name published," the district attorney and "other officials who claimed to have received their information direct from the district attorney's office"—all of whom were speculating on the jury deliberation, evidence in the case and other matters.[109] Such aggressive news gathering was no longer unusual. In fact, the degree to which court reporters were becoming an institutionalized appendage to the judiciary may be indicated by the fact that at least by 1892, New York reporters had their own room in the courthouse.[110]

What Sources Did Reporters Use?

News gathering can fundamentally be defined as the selection and use of sources. It is important, therefore, to examine the sources used by newspaper court reporters as indirect evidence of how they do their jobs and what change may have occurred over time. A close reading of the primary sources suggests the following categories.

Documents and court clerks. Although nominally different, these sources are integrally related since clerks are the primary custodians of court documents. Further, it is generally impossible to determine when clerks themselves are the sources of news stories since they are virtually never named. In fact, I found no example of a court clerk being named as a source in any of the stories read for this study. Yet it is clerks who are in the position to provide access to documents and alert reporters to possibly newsworthy material. Thus it is always possible that when a document has clearly been used, a clerk may have directly or indirectly been involved.

It may be fair to conclude that documents were the very first sources used by the American press in reporting on judicial activity. For example, in 1704 the *Boston News-Letter* published verbatim a governor's proclamation calling for the apprehension of a counterfeiter.[111] Clearly, in 1724, the *Boston Gazette* used a deposition given by a man who had been captured by pirates.[112] In 1774, the *Boston Evening Post* directly quoted a jury verdict.[113] In fact, it seems reasonable to conclude that documents were the source for many of the one- and two-sentence newspaper items listing the disposition of cases—both in the eighteenth and nineteenth centuries.[114]

In sum, there is no reason further to belabor the point that journalists have long used all types of court documents as sources.

Judges. Judges appeared seldom as sources in news stories; when they did appear, it was generally to explain or clarify something. For example, for a *New York Tribune* story on rumors of Tweed Ring indictments, a judge told a reporter he did not know of any indictments nor had he asked the grand jury to reconsider any vote.[115] And a judge in Chicago explained to a reporter why he temporarily stopped turning property over to receivers.[116] But another judge in Chicago was unresponsive to a reporter's questions about his official role in naming an election commissioner, and declared himself "not interviewable."[117]

I found no clear examples of any judge being used as a source until the 1870s.

Prosecuting attorneys. Prosecuting attorneys began to appear commonly as sources at about the middle of the nineteenth century. They appear to have been relatively cooperative sources. For example, in 1872 a New York district attorney told a reporter he was ready to go to trial in a criminal case.[118] Another prosecutor told a *New York Evening Post* reporter that he didn't expect to prove much by a particular witness's forthcoming testimony but that "I think that the case has been well proved already."[119] In Chicago, a *Tribune* reporter reported speculation about the strength of the evidence in a grand jury probe and added that "these rumors all originated in and about the state's attorney's office and are no doubt well-founded."[120] There is also evidence that by the turn of the twentieth century, prosecutors were beginning to make use of news conferences or news releases. According to a story in the *New York Evening Post*:

> Assistant District Attorney Garvan announced today that subpoenas had been served on several persons who were relied on to throw light on the Pulitzer murder case, and that sworn statements would be obtained from them.[121]

Other attorneys. Criminal defense attorneys and civil practice attorneys began to appear as sources about the same time as judges and prosecutors. For example, in 1872, a *New York Tribune* reporter covering a major civil action over possession of a large estate noted that

> it is now claimed by lawyers familiar with the issue that by escheat in default of heirs, the estate is really the property of the State of New York. At any rate it is a subject of discussion among lawyers.[122]

Apparently attorneys were reasonably cooperative sources, and it was not unusual for reporters during and after the 1870s to contact attorneys on both sides of disputes for their comments and opinions,[123] although occasionally an attorney would decline to comment.[124] There is even evidence that by the turn of the century, some private attorneys were holding news conferences. For example, the *New York Tribune* reported that

> William Klein, lawyer for Miss Gibson, returned to New York last night, and stated on the Rialto that he would enter suit for his client in a day or two in the Supreme Court against Albert B. Pierce for $200,000 damages [for malicious prosecution].[125]

No unambiguous examples of attorneys as sources were found in the eighteenth-century American press.

Litigants/criminal defendants. A. M. Lee has noted that after the Civil War, interviewing became something of a mania and that reporters immediately called on anyone who had been guilty of a crime or extraordinary act.[126] Reporters' use of litigants as sources tends to confirm such a conclusion. In fact, such interviewing predates the Civil War. In 1856, a *New York Herald* story noted that

> one of our reporters made another visit to the French prisoners arrested on suspicion of being implicated in the extensive fraud committed in France, of which we have already given a detailed account.[127]

The prisoners responded to the charges and denied them. But by the early 1870s, such interviewing had indeed become common.

Thus in 1872, a *New York Tribune* reporter hastened to interview Mayor Hall after his indictment in the Tweed scandal.[128] Likewise, *Chica-*

go Tribune reporters used such sources as county commissioners who had been indicted for irregularities,[129] a man accused of questionable actions as a bankruptcy receiver,[130] a man accused of murder,[131] and the plaintiff and defendant in a suit over possession of a store.[132] The *New York Herald* quoted those involved in a dispute over an estate,[133] and the *Philadelphia Public Ledger* interviewed interested parties in a dispute over party designation on a ballot.[134]

In sum, newspapers after the middle of the nineteenth century did not hesitate to contact the parties involved in legal disputes, and apparently these sources were frequently quite cooperative.

Jurors. There is also little doubt that newspapers in the nineteenth century used jurors—both petit and grand—as sources, albeit infrequently. And again, it appears that jurors were reasonably cooperative.

For example, already in 1836, the *New York Herald* appeared to have had a source within the jury deciding the infamous Robinson-Jewett murder case. The *Herald* described some of the discussion during jury deliberation.[135] But the use of such sources became relatively more common later in the nineteenth century. Thus in 1886, a *Herald* reporter interviewed members of a jury which had been unable to agree in a bribery case.[136] Later, the *New York Tribune* directly quoted a member of a jury that couldn't agree in an alienation of affection case:

> William Churchill, a juror, said William Bley, another juror, had refused to find any verdict except for the defendant because of the testimony that there was no such room at the Waldorf Astoria as No. 49, which, according to a witness, had been on many occasions occupied by Hanson and Mrs. Carnes under the name of "Dr. Walton and wife."[137]

As evidence that grand jurors were occasionally sources, there is a *New York Tribune* story in 1872 noting that "the evidence which was submitted to the Grand Jury [in the Tweed Ring cases] is of the most startling and conclusive character. There are good reasons why the facts in detail should not be published."[138] The reporter could not resist discussing some of the details, however. Of course, such information could have come from the prosecuting attorney or from witnesses. That seems less likely, however, in a *Chicago Tribune* story which reported that a sitting grand jury was critical of the state's attorney for his handling of a case. The story included quotes from what the attorney had told the jury and discussed some of the jury's internal politics.[139]

Miscellaneous sources. One final indicator of the range of sources used by reporters covering the judiciary is the use of sources more tangentially related to court cases. For example, the *Philadelphia Public Ledger* in 1867 reported direct quotation from a conversation a defendant had had with his sister.[140] A reasonable inference would be that the sister was the source. The *New York Herald*, covering a matricide trial, had a reporter interviewing friends and acquaintances of the victim's family.[141] And the *Herald* went to shocking lengths when covering the case of a broker who had been arrested for bouncing a check to pay for a hotel room during an allegedly adulterous stay. A reporter approached the broker's wife and asked whether she knew who the other woman was and whether she planned a divorce.[142]

The use of these kinds of sources may not have been common, but it illustrates how active and aggressive reporters had become by the second half of the nineteenth century.

Finally, a word should be said about law enforcement authorities as sources. This study is generally confined to the use of sources within the judicial branch itself; but obviously law enforcement officials must have been valuable sources for early court reporters. Although they are not highly visible as sources in many court stories, they must have played a significant background role in coloring reporters' perceptions of defendants' guilt, in providing background information on defendants and the incidents which led to the charges against them, and in providing access to defendants for such purposes as interviewing.

Few stories provide so obviously the evidence of this as a *New York Herald* report that a police inspector had announced a murder suspect's confession and invited the press to interview the culprit.[143] But when, for example, one reads in the *Chicago Tribune* that a man accused of murder "was erroneously classed as a gambler, as in fact he has been merely a confidence man and common thief," that it seems "marvelous" that anyone could sympathize with him, and that he is a "desperado," are not police the most logical source for such a perception?[144]

Bias, Color and Style

Court reporting in the eighteenth century was frank, to the point and reasonably detached. An example from the *Boston News-Letter* is representative:

> On Monday and Tuesday last, a Special Court of Admiralty was held here, for the Tryal of Piracy, &c. wherein Fifteen Persons (being forc'd Men) were Acquitted and Discharged: Four others were found Guilty and received Sentence of Death, viz. William Fly, Capt. (who also is to be hung in Chains) Samuel Cole, Quarter Master, George Condick, and Henry Greenville.[145]

When such reporting departed from our contemporary concept of objectivity, it often did so with a moralistic twist. For example, the *New York Gazette*, covering the trial and sentencing of a black man for attempting to ravish (rape), concluded by noting that

> by the inspection of the Justice [a burn] inflicted on this Negro, it is hoped it may be a Means to deter others from attempting such wicked crimes in the future.[146]

The *Boston News-Letter* referred to the discovery of a counterfeiting and the commencement of proceedings against suspects as a "favorable smile of Providence to this Province."[147] And the *Boston Evening Post* ventured so far as to remark, upon the arrest of several counterfeiters, that "our Gallows has groaned for him [one of the suspects] a long Time."[148]

But such blatant statements were more the exception than the rule. In fact, even William Duane of the partisan *Philadelphia Aurora* occasionally went out of his way to be neutral. Once, while reporting on a case involving an assault on the editor himself, he wrote that

> as it is our wish in the case to give the whole of this transaction in as impartial a manner as possible, we have postponed the detail of this trial until the report of the evidence shall be duly and correctly authenticated in the most minute way.[149]

A week later, when he did provide the full report, he reprinted a story from another newspaper "rather than risk any danger of misconception, which as a party in the case we might involuntarily fall into."[150]

Even during and after the penny press days of the nineteenth century, much court reporting was surprisingly neutral and balanced.[151] Much court reporting was presented in lists or short items indicating the status or disposition of cases. Items from the *New York Evening Post* and the *New York Tribune* are representative: .

> The Delaware Bank vs. James Andrews.—This was an action of trover brought to recover $950, transmitted in a package on the 17th of February, 1841, to the American Exchange bank in this city, which never reached the latter institution.[152]

> In the Court of Common Pleas an action was brought by Amasa Hathaway against Henry Ogden to recover the amount of a note for $225.—The plea of usury was set up, a little more than 7 per cent. having been charged in discounting it. There was also a deposit as collateral, of some Shawangunk Mining Company stock, but it has become worthless. The jury found for defendant.[153]

There are also examples of newspapers striving to correct wrong impressions, such as when the *Public Ledger* noted that

> the arrest of Mr. Theodore Kerns on Saturday morning at Franklin and Coates Streets, on what were, deemed suspicious circumstances, has been satisfactorily explained, and relieves him from any charge of impropriety. He has always borne a good character.[154]

In fact, a great deal of the court reporting from the 1830s on was as much stenography as it was journalism. For example, the *New York Tribune* one day in 1842 devoted five full columns to coverage of a forgery trial. But the reporter contributed little more than an opening paragraph setting the scene:

The Court-Room was crowded to suffocation at a very early hour this morning, and more excitement was manifest within and around its doors than has attended any trial since that of the murderer Colt. Considerable confusion prevailed as so large a crowd had evidently not been expected. The prisoner looked on with a smile of apparent scorn, and appeared quite indifferent to the preparations for his trial.[155]

Coverage continued for five more days and filled another twenty-six columns; the reporting was virtually all verbatim.[156]

Of course, there were excesses. Sometimes—most notably in police court reporting—color became more important than substance, and literary license took over.[157] For example:

Robert H. Howe was charged with committing an assault upon James M'Duffie and wife. It appeared M'Duffie and his lady had retired to their chamber in a tavern, on Sunday evening, and not dreaming that their midnight bliss was threatened with nullification, left the door unlocked. Howe, who had been accommodated with a liberal discount from the bar, and his heart inclining unto evil, disencumbered his heels of their shoes, and stealthily ascended the stairs and glided into the earthly paradise. Having "advanced his miscreated front" to the hymeneal couch, he acquainted the lady with the object of his unexpected visit; but . . .[158]

It is worth noting that reporters were not the only ones to take literary license. The *Boston Transcript* in 1841 reported on a trial for keeping a disorderly dancehall, and quoted a prosecuting attorney who said he wished he had known sooner that a particular witness was a musician at the dancehall since he

would have been able to have brought more fully to the knowledge of the jury all of the crotchets, flats and sharps, ad libitum passages, and libertine con amore notes, which were scored down literally in that place.[159]

Not all examples of color are as relatively innocuous. A *Chicago Tribune* reporter, noting the acquittal of a defendant in a swindling case, called the swindle "one of the most impudent . . . of which we have ever heard," and confessed that he was "at a loss to understand" how the jurors could have acquitted.[160] A *New York Tribune* reporter, describing jury selection in a criminal trial, wrote that

the session was extremely dull and uninteresting, save at occasional moments when the unusual stupidity of one juror or the attempted smartness of another provoked the mirth of the spectators.[161]

Another *Tribune* story, this one on the arraignment of a man for grand larceny, noted that the defendant "has a bad record, but has managed to keep out of prison until now."[162] Yet another *Tribune* story, a report of a murder trial, described those waiting in the courtroom as "the worst looking crowd that has ever been seen in the General Sessions Building. Nearly all the men were friends of the prisoner or members of the gang which haunts the winter racetracks."[163] And a *New York Evening Post* reporter blatantly inserted his own conclusions regarding the merits of an accused forger's insanity defense:

> Field [the defendant] sat throughout the proceedings in a listless attitude, leaning his head on his hand, his eyes closed, and apparently sleeping. His hair appeared not to have been brushed for some time, and he did not remove his overcoat, the collar of which remained turned up. His whole air was that of a man too crushed longer to care what his fate might be. To the superficial eye, there was no indication of insanity.[164]

It may be that such reporting led to the public disorder that occurred during some nineteenth-century criminal trials.[165]

Criticism

Newspaper court reporting, particularly in the nineteenth century, was not uncriticized, but with some notable exceptions, the criticism centered more on questions of taste than on questions of fairness or interference with fair trials.

Critics within the press. Police court reporting was soundly criticized within the newspaper community as soon as it appeared. And the criticism has a contemporary ring. Already in 1828, some New York newspapers were complaining that

> it [police court reporting] is a fashion which does not meet with our approbation, on the score of either propriety or taste. To say nothing of the absolute indecency of some of the cases which are allowed occasionally to creep into print, we deem it of little benefit to the cause of morals thus to familiarize the community, and especially the younger parts of it, to the details of misdemeanor and crime. . . . Besides, it suggests to the novice in vice all the means of becoming expert in its devices.[166]

Similar complaints surfaced in Boston when the *Spectator* lamented that the penny papers were promoting licentiousness and corrupting young people.[167] The *Boston Transcript* suggested that some penny press court coverage was garbage.[168] Greeley, in 1841, complained that court reporting was becoming reckless, unprincipled and immoral under the hypocritical pretense that the press was duty-bound to keep the public informed.[169] Bennett and his aggressive *New York Herald* became the target of a "moral war."[170]

Ironically, the *Boston Transcript*, one of the critics, itself became a heavy user of police court reports and justified its behavior on grounds that it was reducing crime.[171] And the *Boston Times* defended itself by asserting that many potential criminals might fear press publicity more than punishment.[172]

Critics from without. Some of the angriest published criticism came in

1859 from Lambert Wilmer, himself once a journalist. Wilmer's was also some of the first published criticism to complain that court reporting interfered with the administration of justice.[173] He also accused journalists of frequently accepting bribes from criminals in exchange for favorable publicity.[174] Unfortunately, Wilmer is as weak on evidence as he is strong on rhetoric, and substantially rests his case on the logic that

> the more probable a story is, the less proof is required. This allegation against the editors is so extremely probable, that I defy you, or any other man or woman, to point out any reason why it should be doubted.[175]

Other critics apparently took more direct action. About 1880, George Ochs, then a 22-year-old reporter for the *Chattanooga Times*, was told by a county official that he would "shoot him full of holes" if Ochs printed his name in connection with a divorce. The story was printed. A few days later, the official attacked him on the street with a cane; Ochs pulled a pistol and shot him in the abdomen, then put the gun to the man's throat and pulled the trigger, but the gun jammed.[176] After the *New York Herald* printed a story about a woman who signed a blank check given her by her father for more than he allowed, the woman horsewhipped the reporter and was arrested for that.[177] The *Herald* also reported an attempted horsewhipping of a reporter who had written about a woman's trial and acquittal on bigamy charges. She never did succeed in seeing the reporter, but complained to others that "he was constantly associating her name with every scandal that occurred, and she proposed to stop it."[178]

During the last quarter of the nineteenth century, legal journals—still a relatively new type of publication—began to contain comment critical of the press. The criticism centered primarily on inaccuracies and poor taste but began to address fair trial issues. For example, in 1875 the *Albany Law Journal* bitterly attacked press coverage of a case because of its "nasty" facts.[179] "Some countries have been ruined because they were priest-ridden," the author wrote. "We stand in some danger of being ruined because we are press-ridden. Ignorance, violence, prejudice, partiality, even venality, characterize many of these men in their treatment of legal matters."[180] Further, "it has become almost impossible for a public man to have a fair trial in this country, because of the fear of newspapers."[181]

A year later, the *Central Law Journal*, published in St. Louis, complained that

> those daily and weekly newspapers which occasionally report the transactions of the courts, usually employ their general local reporters, men who are not lawyers, have never had a legal training, and who have about the same idea of the distinction between a bond and a writ, that the apprentice in Pickwick had of the difference between oxalic acid and epsom salts.[182]

And in the mid-1880s, the *American Law Review* sarcastically noted that the secular newspapers hardly ever attempt to report a judicial trial without making egregious blunders, unless they employ a stenographer and take down every word, including the dictum of the judge to the janitor to put some more coal in the stove; and they hardly ever undertake to criticize a judicial trial without making the same spectacle of themselves.[183]

By 1892, an attorney was stating flatly in *Criminal Law Magazine* that "it has become a question of trial by newspaper or trial by the law of the land, and trial by newspaper is trial without law."[184]

Libel actions and exercises of the contempt power against newspapers may also be regarded as criticism of press coverage, but those topics are addressed below.

DISCUSSION

Two questions must now be considered: (1) What factors may have combined to produce the type of court reporting done during the eighteenth and nineteenth centuries? and (2) What do the findings of this historical research suggest about the newsmaking process?

Influences

Clearly, many factors may have affected the way newspaper court reporting developed, but I shall focus on four—society's general attitudes about deviance and how best to deal with it; the nature of the bench and bar; legal controls, more specifically libel and contempt; and journalists' concept of objectivity.

Attitudes.   Evidence about people's attitudes about crime in the eighteenth and nineteenth centuries is extremely difficult to find. But at least two general conclusions have been drawn: first, people's concept of crime changed from one of sin to one of crime as environmentally caused; second and concomitantly, as this concept changed, the acceptance of the need to place offenders in institutions grew.

David Rothman, who studied the emergence of asylum treatment in the United States, writes that eighteenth-century Americans didn't think poverty and crime indicated a defect in community organization or that they could be eliminated through ameliorative action.[185] Legal historian Lawrence Friedman agrees, noting that as late as 1774 crime was regarded as synonymous with sin. Thus, he maintains, trials were actually status degradation ceremonies, and since the goal of punishment was "to reteach and retouch the erring soul . . . it used, as means to this end, confession, public humiliation, and infamy."[186]

But as the nineteenth century began, population began to explode; the number of urban residents, bolstered by immigration, mushroomed.

And with population growth and urbanization came an increase in violent and property crime. Modern urban police systems were created beginning in the 1830s in large part in reaction to a period of great urban violence.[187] The days of the old "watch-and-ward" system were over, and New York, Boston and Philadelphia led the way in developing police systems.[188] Consequently,

> people detested crime and were afraid of it. They wanted bad people kept out of sight and circulation. Despite the rhetoric, the evidence of what men did shows that they considered it more important to warehouse, quarantine and guard the "criminal" than to cure them of their criminal habits. People were skeptical, moreover, whether it was possible to make these criminals over.[189]

Not surprisingly, much of the criminal law could be characterized as "blunt, merciless and swift."[190] Concepts of due process of law were only beginning to take form, and the states were not bound by the federal Bill of Rights. And when the checks and balances in the legal system ran too far ahead of public opinion, the public was willing to take the law into its own hands.[191] As one scholar puts it, a "Who's Who of American Vigilantism" would include U.S. senators and congressmen, governors, judges, wealthy businessmen, generals, lawyers, and even clergymen. "In those days [the nineteenth century] leading men were often prominent members of vigilante movements and proud of it."[192]

In any case, once the American concept of crime had changed from sin related to environment related, Americans may have been more interested in achieving the end of institutionalizing deviants than in the means by which they did so. As Rothman maintains, "after a few decades officials interpreted the mere presence of men in cells as itself valuable."[193]

Seen against this general background, much about newspaper court reporting seems understandable. If eighteenth-century Americans regarded crime as sin and saw the judicial process as status degradation, it is understandable that newspapers were willing to publicize even such distasteful activities as incest or infanticide. Such publicity might have been seen as merely part of the cleansing process. Also understandable is the moralizing that was occasionally found in court stories. Indeed, the discovery and punishment of a deviant act might be reasonably regarded as a favorable sign of Providence and as a useful example to others.

Nor is it surprising that court reporting should have expanded in quantity and color in the nineteenth century. Obviously, more was available to report. But it is striking that highly colorful reporting—such as police court reporting—took root not only when police courts themselves were created but during a time when crime was being perceived as a truly secular problem. Sin is no laughing matter; but it may seem somehow less harmful to poke fun when the subject has been a victim of environmental factors instead of trouble with the Deity. It may be, too, that the anonymity provided by a growing urban environment made it easier to poke fun at one's fellows with relative impunity.

It is also possible to understand the color and occasional outrageous bias in nineteenth-century court reporting, and the relative lack of criticism of interference with fair trial throughout much of the century. If Americans were fearful of crime in a violent era during which due process rights were not strongly and specifically established, what could be wrong with publicity that, at worst, might assist in getting undesirables off the streets and into institutions for possible rehabilitation? This may be a doubly plausible explanation if one accepts Hughes's assertion that "readers as a rule do not identify criminals' lives with their own and do not resent their getting publicity."[194]

Bench and bar. As noted at the beginning of this chapter, the legal profession was not highly regarded at the beginning of the eighteenth century. But the profession apparently did little to police and improve itself. There were no bar associations setting standards of ethics and competence. If anything, during the first half of the nineteenth century, requirements for bar admission were relaxed, in part because of the still prevailing distrust of the profession and in part as another ramification of Jacksonian democracy.[195] In fact, in the 1840s, some states eliminated all requirements except good moral character for admission to the bar.[196] The American lawyer was a man of action and cunning, not scholarship.[197] One scholar of the history of the legal profession has flatly concluded that "for more than a hundred years after the Revolution, no adequate examining machinery existed [for admission to the bar] in any state."[198] What few bar clubs and associations did exist in the early nineteenth century did nothing to provide cohesion or self-control.[199]

Meanwhile, almost all lawyers were constantly looking for new business, and although they did use newspaper advertising, word of mouth may have been more important.[200] As Friedman puts it, "Eloquence in court gained attention, and attention gained clients."[201] That, in turn, meant that courts provided entertainment as well as justice.[202] According to one law professor, "The criminal trial was the theatre and spectaculum of old rural America. Applause and cat calls were not infrequent. All too easily lawyers and judges became part-time actors at the bar."[203] Friedman agrees that judges, too, became involved, that their charges to juries sometimes ran to enormous length and that they "expatiated on subjects far distant from the business at hand."[204]

Only after the Civil War did new bar organizations begin to focus on ethics, primarily because corruption within the profession had become staggering and extended to judges as well as attorneys.[205] Even so, the first formal ethical code wasn't adopted until 1887; the American Bar Association adopted its code of ethics in 1908.[206]

Several conclusions seem warranted. First, the nature of the bar in the nineteenth century may at least partially explain why prosecutors, defense attorneys and other attorneys cooperated with the press outside of the courtroom; the great distaste for the legal profession in the eighteenth century may also partially explain why attorneys virtually never overtly appear as sources in newspaper stories then. Second, the colorful style of court reporting that emerged with the penny press may be quite understandable in light of the nature of the bar and bench; that is, colorful attorneys, judges and litigants may have lent themselves exceedingly well to that type of coverage. And attorneys needing publicity certainly found it in the descriptive portions and even in the verbatim portions of nineteenth century court stories. Third, the lack of standards of either competence or ethics for attorneys may also partially explain why there are so few examples of conflicts over fair trial versus free press. Conversely, the growing concern within the legal profession about ethics and qualifications that emerged in the last third of the nineteenth century helps explain why the bar began complaining about the press more loudly then, both on fair trial and taste grounds.

In sum, conditions during much of the nineteenth century must have lent themselves perfectly to court reporting which could attract an interested audience and perhaps please many in the bar and bench.

Legal controls: contempt and libel.   The evidence suggests that neither contempt nor libel was a serious problem for the press as it reported on courts, although the specter of both must have been always present.

The earliest evidence of a newspaper reporter encountering the threat of contempt for merely publishing an account of an open court proceeding came in 1830 during the Knapp murder trial in Salem, Mass.[207] In that case,

> The Chief Justice remarked that there seemed to be an intention of publishing in the newspapers, the proceedings of the Court from day to day. Such publications must necessarily be imperfect, and perhaps mischievous. The Court is, therefore, decidedly of opinion that the proceedings ought not be thus published as they would give only imperfect information. What passes one day may be essentially altered or modified by the doings of a subsequent day. There may be no objection to publishing the state of the case as it advances; but there must be no publication of the evidence before the trials are concluded.[208]

The court's attempt at control, however, was decidedly ineffective. James Gordon Bennett, who was covering the trial for the *New York Courier and Enquirer*, published a strong attack on the state's attorney and the court for making the effort, and the press generally ignored the judges.[209] After a day, the judges officially reopened court, with the rather odd proviso that reporters were to take no notes.[210]

Meanwhile, legislation was being adopted to limit the power of state and federal courts to punish for constructive contempt. Pennsylvania led the way in 1809 with a law specifying that out-of-court publications concerning participants in a pending proceeding should not be construed or punished as contempt.[211] New York, 20 years later, adopted a law providing that "no court can punish as a contempt, the publication of true, full and fair reports of any trial, argument, proceedings or decision had in such court."[212] Two years later, Congress limited the contempt power of the federal courts:

> the power of the several courts of the United States to issue attachments and inflict summary punishments for contempt of court, shall not be construed to extend to any cases except the misbehaviour of any person or persons in the presence of the said courts, or so near thereto as to obstruct the administration of justice.[213]

By 1860, twenty-three of the then thirty-three states had implemented similar policies.[214]

The evidence suggests that throughout the nineteenth century, contempt was a problem for journalists who published critical comment about the judiciary, but not for journalists merely covering court cases as spot news. Further, when conflicts did arise, the press appears to have been generally cooperative. For example, a federal court at the beginning of a criminal trial in 1842 ordered that, although it could not punish publication as contempt, "no person will be allowed to come within the bar of the court for the purpose of reporting, except on condition of suspending all publication till after the trial is concluded."[215] On that condition, the court agreed to provide space for reporters; consequently, "the reporters expressed their acquiescence . . . and the most respectful silence, on the part of the press, prevailed during the whole trial."[216] In 1854, a Kentucky state judge ordered the press not to publish testimony during a murder trial, and the press agreed.[217]

The *Chicago Tribune* apparently flirted with trouble during the 1855 trial of several persons involved in a riot. A defense attorney asked the court to order the newspaper to show cause why it should not be held in contempt and prohibited from further reporting on the case because an article on the case contained false statements about the defendants and was disrespectful of their character. The *Tribune* reporter, by the court's permission, stood up, offered to correct any factual errors and stated that "the article was written to advance the ends of justice."[218] Then:

> The Court remarked that it was very wrong for newspapers to publish articles which may influence the result of the trial one way or another; and that it was very desirable that if any reports at all were published, that they should be simple relations of facts as they occurred. He hoped that if the matter were now dropped, the reporter would be careful in the future to make his reports correct.
>
> The matter was then informally passed over.[219]

No one can know how frequently such incidents occurred,[220] but there is little evidence that nineteenth-century reporters were troubled with contempt for reporting on open court proceedings.[221]

The nature of the contempt power, thus, may have had significant implications for the development of newspaper court reporting. In the eighteenth century, when the contempt power of judges was relatively unlimited, there is no indicatiion that court reporting was affected. Of course, it might be argued that one reason so much reporting was so concise and generally disposition-oriented is fear of judicial intervention. This, however, seems unlikely since eighteenth-century court reporting does not seem to have been qualitatively different from other types of local reporting and since it is likely that court records themselves were the source of many court stories. The availability of the contempt power, plus the potential for seditious libel prosecution, may have kept the press more docile than it would have otherwise been; nevertheless, this study produced no evidence of the contempt power being used against eighteenth-century editors for mere publication of proceedings in open court.

It is striking that legislative restrictions on the contempt power coincided with the heightened attention to court coverage by the press in the nineteenth century. Certainly, such legislation removed a possibly serious impediment to the more colorful, descriptive and detailed reporting that began to develop, and may have made it easier for reporters actively to pursue judicial stories outside of the courtroom. Nor is there any indication that reporting was affected even when judges began to bypass contempt statutes later in the century.[222] Such a conclusion applies to investigative, as well as spot news, reporting.

In sum, the contempt power probably did not negatively affect court reporting either in the eighteenth or nineteenth centuries, although there may have been an intangible inhibiting effect. The legislative protection from constructive contempt beginning in the early 1800s may have provided protection that allowed a new, more active and aggressive type of court reporting to evolve.

The press may have had somewhat more difficulty with libel; however, nineteenth-century developments in libel law probably removed a potential impediment to the evolution of reporting.

There is no evidence that libel suits were a problem for eighteenth-century American newspapers reporting on court proceedings, although the qualified privilege had not yet developed. Even during the first half of the nineteenth century, when a colorful and sometimes licentious type of court reporting developed, few libel cases were reported.[223] There may have been unreported cases, however, since Hudson writes that as Bennett grew wealthy with his *New York Herald*, he became the target of "frivolous cases, made out of police reports, and instituted by speculating lawyers."[224] Hudson also notes that Bennett "employed abundance of counsel, and fought these cases, in the general interest of the Press, as long as the law would permit, [doing] more by this mode, in stopping these vexatious suits than by all the changes in the law of libel."[225] Unfortunately, Hudson tells us nothing of the disposition of these cases.

Bennett and his fellow publishers must have been helped, however, by the passage in 1854 of a New York state law specifying that

> no reporter, editor or proprietor of any newspaper shall be liable to any action . . . for a fair and true report . . . of any judicial, legislative, or other public official proceeding.[226]

Nelson believes this law reflects a codification of the common law of privilege which had been developing in England and, apparently, in the United States, since the turn of the nineteenth century.[227] In England, the birth of the common law regarding qualified privilege to report judicial proceedings has been generally traced to 1796.[228] In the United States, the recognition of the privilege roughly coincided with the rise of the penny press,[229] although it was an 1884 decision which is credited as perhaps the first clear statement of the rationale for such a privilege.[230]

Despite statutory and common-law protection, newspaper libel suits became more numerous in the latter half of the nineteenth century, but there is no way of knowing how many suits were filed over court stories.[231] Edwin Shuman, in a reporting textbook published in 1903, was clearly concerned about frivolous but expensive libel actions:

> The average cost of defending a suit is $500. The Philadelphia Times [founded in 1875] once states that it had paid more than $20,000 for the defense of libel suits in the first thirteen years of its career, though the verdict was for the paper in every case.[232]

Again, however, there is no way of knowing whether any of these suits stemmed from court reporting.

In sum, there is reason to believe that the development of libel law was a factor in the development of newspaper court reporting. The potential severity of the law in the eighteenth century before development of qualified privilege may well have discouraged more detailed and descriptive court reporting. However, this reasoning should not be pushed too far, particularly since this study uncovered no examples of eighteenth-century newspapers being sued for libel in reports of judicial proceedings despite the fact that some highly defamatory information was published. The development of the defense of qualified privilege in the nineteenth century, however, coincided ideally with the emergence of a mass press and certainly made it possible for newspapers to publish highly interesting but defamatory information about court cases with relative impunity. One might argue that the press received this protection just when it began to need it most. Despite the increase in the number of suits in the second half of the century, there is little evidence that court reporting itself was affected; reporting did not obviously become more conservative. On the contrary, reporters became even more aggressive in their news gathering, and the first investigative reporting on the judicial system began to appear. If there were a "chilling effect," this study was unable to detect it.

Objectivity. Finally, a brief word should be said about the role of reporters' concepts of objectivity. Particularly relevant is the work of Michael Schudson, who convincingly argues that journalists in the nineteenth century (and presumably also in the eighteenth century) had no concept of objectivity as journalists in the twentieth century define it. Schudson believes that until the 1920s, American journalists had no reason to doubt the firmness of the "reality" by which they lived.[233] That is, they believed that facts were clearly observable "aspects of the world" and were not themselves the product of personal subjectivity.[234] There was no perceived distinction between "facts" and "color" in journalists' definition of accuracy.[235] By the 1890s, Schudson argues, reporters saw themselves in part as scientists uncovering the economic and political facts of industrial life more clearly and realistically than anyone had before.[236]

What this suggests is that much of eighteenth- and nineteenth-century reporting that now seems outrageously biased and prejudicial may well not have been so perceived by journalists and their readers at the time. Much of what we now perceive as color may well have been perceived by early journalists as undeniable, objective fact. Thus, for example, the *Chicago Tribune* court reporter in 1855 may have been truly astonished when an attorney complained about inaccuracy and disrespect; and we can begin to understand why the reporter told the judge that his purpose in writing the article was "to advance the ends of justice."[237] Perhaps, too, we can begin to understand more clearly why what criticism there was of early court reporting focused predominantly on taste and later on fair trial, but relatively little on accuracy.

News Making

Certainly, the historical research tells us something about how newspaper court reporting evolved. And I have speculated about some factors that may have been crucial to that evolution. But what does the evidence indicate about the news-making process itself? In chapter 2 I suggested that the idea of exchange behavior is highly useful to an understanding of the reporter-source interaction that produces news. That concept is also useful in analyzing the historical data.

First, it is striking how seldom judges appeared as sources. Of course, this could be because judges seldom had information reporters needed and could not obtain elsewhere; but it could also be that judges had relatively little clear incentive to mingle with reporters. Attorneys—and even litigants—appeared relatively frequently as sources. Again, this could be because they were likely to have information reporters wanted; but it could also be because they wanted publicity for their views. This is especially likely in light of attorneys' need to advertise and in the absence of reasonably clear-cut ethical bounds to extrajudicial comment. Indeed, if the nineteenth-century American attorney were basically a man of cunning and action, he would certainly not have hesitated to make whatever uses possible of newspaper publicity about his case. This may also explain in part why so many litigants—even criminal defendants represented by counsel—were willing to discuss their cases with the press. Perhaps their attorneys were not discouraging this contact with the press, and perhaps they saw a useful opportunity to use publicity about their side to their advantage. Or perhaps, at the very least, they saw no obvious reason why publicity should be harmful.

Second, when judges were quoted by reporters, the information they supplied did seem to be different in character from that supplied by attorneys and litigants. More specifically, judges tended to provide factual information about cases or, at most, explanation about something that had occurred in court. When reporters attempted to probe beyond such points, judges might become "not interviewable."[238] Attorneys and litigants, on the other hand, were more willing to talk about the merits of a case and, in some cases, to defend themselves strongly.

The fact that attorneys and litigants appeared more frequently as sources than did judges may suggest that they had more to gain in the exchange—namely, publicity for their views. Without that incentive (and, concededly, without reporters' needing a great deal of the information judges possessed), judges may have had much less tangible reasons to cooperate. Therefore, with judges having little need for the reporters' major commodity—publicity—and with reporters needing little information that only the judges could provide, the grounds for exchange become limited, and we should not be surprised to see relatively little of judges as sources.[239]

But exchange behavior and the evolution of court reporting have a somewhat reciprocal relationship. One of the findings of the historical research was that journalists slowly but clearly expanded their routine spectrum of news sources and became much more active in gathering information. This movement, particularly in the nineteenth century, must have also put increasing pressure on reporters to develop sound, reliable, cooperative sources. As reporters moved beyond direct observation and inspecting documents as information-gathering techniques, for perhaps the first time their relationships with sources became crucial. The fierce newspaper competition of much of the nineteenth century must have contributed even more pressure.

To develop and cultivate sources, reporters must have consciously and unconsciously developed "commodities" to exchange for that cooperation. Perhaps some of those commodities were at least initially as simple as the reputation of the reporter's newspaper or the mere novelty of receiving a reporter's attention. Whatever they were and however naturally and even unconsciously they might have developed, they contributed to a change in the amount and nature of information that became news. Sources, too, must have felt increasing pressure to cooperate. For example, if attorneys depended in part on publicity for building and maintaining their practices, this must have become more difficult as cities grew, as courts became busier and as newspapers had to be more selective in their attention. If so, this may have been an incentive for attorneys—and even litigants—to cooperate or possibly seek out reporters.

Thus the evolution of court reporting may have influenced the nature of reporter-source relationships, which in turn may have influenced the nature of judicial news. The new importance of these relationships coupled with the movement away from sheerly verbatim reporting of court proceedings must also have begun occasional tugs-of-war in which sources attempted to manipulate reporters and vice versa. It may also have marked the beginning of the problem of news being skewed toward the most accessible, cooperative sources.

Finally, some inferences may be drawn about the implications of reporter and source roles. If one assumes that the most important goal of a source cooperating to obtain manipulative publicity is to obtain publicity which promotes the source's view, then attorneys and litigants should more often than judges act, in Nimmo's terms, as "promoters." Judges should act as "informers" or, at most, "educators." In fact, that is what the historical data suggest. Not one instance was found of a judge acting as a "promoter"; but lawyers and litigants did act in such roles, as, for example, when a prosecutor told a reporter during a trial that he felt his case had been well proved.[240]

Reporters are difficult to categorize. Undoubtedly, those who wrote verbatim accounts of court proceedings would fall into Nimmo's "recorder" type. At the other extreme are those reporters who became blatantly judgmental, and they would seem to fall into the "prescriber" role. Yet these two types—and the intermediate type, the "expositor"—may be exhibited by the same reporter in the same story, as when a lengthy verbatim transcript is introduced by a judgmental sentence or two. Such categorization is further confounded because objectivity did not necessarily mean in the nineteenth century what it does now.

Nevertheless, reporter and source roles are useful analysis tools. As reporters became more aggressive news gatherers, the potential for conflict with sources must have grown. The potential for conflict may also have resulted from some highly embellished, colorful, judgmental reporting. In other words, as reporters ventured out of the recorder role and into more active roles, their relationships with some sources may well have changed from cooperative to compatible or even competitive.[241] Conflict was all the more likely when, as noted above, attorneys and litigants fit into the promoter category. Under such analysis, the emergence of more press criticism by the bar in the latter part of the nineteenth century makes sense. Reporters were stepping beyond the recorder role; attorneys were stepping beyond the informer role; and the bar was becoming more sensitive to ethical considerations. Nor is it surprising that the criticism took on a more practical bent, focusing more and more on the danger of prejudicial publicity—a problem with very direct ramifications for attorneys and clients.

Consideration of roles may also explain in part why judges were less visible sources than attorneys. Again, if judges were acting primarily as informers or educators while reporters were stepping into more active roles, judges may have become reluctant sources.

SUMMARY

This chapter has provided historical context until now lacking in the study of newspaper court reporting. Primary and secondary sources were used to examine the development of court reporting in the eighteenth and nineteenth centuries, with particular attention to who reporters were, what sources they used, how they did their jobs and how they wrote. The findings show that newspapers even in the eighteenth century gave considerable attention to local court proceedings but that reporters in the nineteenth century became far more active, particularly in pursuing sources outside of court proceedings themselves. Nineteenth-century court reporting was extensive, often relying on lengthy verbatim stenographic reports. Color and bias did appear in some stories, but much of the reporting in the eighteenth and nineteenth centuries was objective, even by today's standards. I suggested that public attitudes about deviance, the nature of the bench and bar, developments in the law of libel and contempt and even reporters' concept of objectivity influenced the development of court reporting. Finally, the evidence was considered in light of the exchange model of reporter-source interaction and in the context of reporter and source roles.

Notes

1. "The Witch Walpurga is Tried and Sentenced for Her Wanton Rendezvous with the Devil," quoted in Louis L. Snyder and Richard B. Morris, eds., *A Treasury of Great Reporting* (New York: Simon & Schuster, 1949), p. 2.

2. Matthias A. Shaaber, *Some Forerunners of the Newspaper in England* (Philadelphia: University of Pennsylvania Press, 1929), pp. 141–42. For an example of a ballad, see Helen M. Hughes, *News and the Human Interest Story* (Chicago: University of Chicago Press, 1940), pp. 138–40.

3. Shaaber, pp. 250–52.

4. Ibid., pp. 252–53.

5. *Mercurius Politicus*, 26 June–3 July 1656, cited by Joseph Frank, *The Beginnings of the English Newspaper*, 1620–1660 (Cambridge: Harvard University Press, 1961), unnumbered insert.

6. Frank, pp. 81–82.

7. Ibid, p. 226.

8. *Universal Spectator and Weekly Journal*, 23 September 1732, cited by Willard G. Bleyer, *Main Currents in the History of American Journalism* (New York: Houghton Mifflin, 1927), pp. 32–33.

9. Ted Peterson, "British Crime Pamphleteers: Forgotten Journalists," *Journalism Quarterly* 22 (1945):310–13.

10. Ibid., p. 316.

11. John Wight, *Mornings at Bow Street* (London: D.S. Maurice, 1824).

12. Alexander Andrews, *The History of British Journalism*, 2 vols. (London: Richard Bentley, 1859), 2:182–83.

13. Wight, pp. iv–v.

14. Matthias A. Shaaber, "Forerunners of the Newspaper in America," *Journalism Quarterly* 11 (1934):340.

15. Ibid., p. 346.

16. *Boston News-Letter*, 27 October–3 November 1729.

17. See, e.g., James W. Carey, "The Problem of Journalism History," *Journalism History* 1 (1974):3–5.

18. Bleyer; Frank L. Mott, *American Journalism*, 3d ed. (New York: Macmillan, 1962); Edwin Emery and Michael Emery, *The Press and America*, 4th ed. (Englewood Cliffs, N.J.: Prentice-Hall, 1978). Final selections were made in personal consultation with Prof. Edwin Emery of the University of Minnesota School of Journalism and Mass Communication.

19. As a further check for possible regional differences, issues of the *South Carolina Gazette* and the *Atlanta Constitution* were randomly examined. No obvious regional variation was suggested. Joseph Pulitzer's *New York World* was also checked randomly for obvious differences in reporting technique and coverage. No such differences appeared.

20. It was also important to read more colonial newspapers because local courts met irregularly, making it likely that a random sample would miss too much. An attempt to reduce the number of papers read by examining only those issues published on or immediately after dates courts were supposed to be in session was not successful. The correspondence was too inconsistent.

21. Lawrence M. Friedman, *A History of American Law* (New York: Simon & Schuster, 1973), p. 81.

22. Roscoe Pound, *Organization of Courts* (Boston: Little, Brown & Co., 1940), p. 28.

23. Ibid.

24. Friedman, pp. 32–42.

25. Francis H. Heller, *The Sixth Amendment to the Constitution of the United States* (Lawrence: University of Kansas Press, 1951), p. 15.

26. See, e.g., Anna M. Kross and Harold M. Grossman, "Magistrates Courts of the City of New York: History and Organization," *Brooklyn Law Review* 7 (1937):133–79; Frank M. Eastman, *Courts and Lawyers of Pennsylvania: 1623–1923* (New York: American Historical Society, 1922); Emory Washburn, *Sketches of the Judicial History of Massachusetts: 1630–1775* (Boston: Little and Brown,

1840); William T. Davis, *History of the Judiciary of Massachusetts* (Boston: Boston Book Company, 1900); Julius Goebel, Jr., and T. Raymond Naughton, *Law Enforcement in Colonial New York: A Study in Criminal Procedure* (New York: Commonwealth Fund, 1944).

27. Ibid.

28. Goebel and Naughton, pp. 339–54. In petty cases, the magistrate or justice of the peace could make an immediate judgment.

29. Ibid., p. 574.

30. Reprinted in Richard L. Perry and John C. Cooper, eds., *Sources of Our Liberties: Documentary Origins of Individual Liberties in the United States Constitution and Bill of Rights* (New York: American Bar Foundation, 1959), pp. 156, 153.

31. Ibid., p. 217.

32. Ibid., p. 188.

33. Ibid., p. 366; Francis H. Thorpe, *The Federal and State Constitutions, Colonial Charters, and Other Organic Laws of the States, Territories, and Colonies, Now or Heretofore Forming the United States of America* (H.R. Doc. 357, 59th Cong., 2d sess., 1909), 5:3083; 1:569; 5:2787.

34. Gilbert Geis, "Preliminary Hearings and the Press," *UCLA Law Review* 8 (1961):406–407. By contrast, preliminary hearings in England were closed until the mid-nineteenth century—even to the accused and his attorney. Ibid., pp. 400–01. Although there was some movement in the United States in the mid-nineteenth century to avoid prejudicial publicity by closing preliminary hearings, at least at the defendant's request, stringent closure rules were never universally adopted. Ibid., pp. 407–09.

35. Bleyer, p. 74.

36. Sidney Kobre, *The Development of the Colonial Newspaper* (Pittsburgh: Colonial Press, 1944), p. 21.

37. Mott, p. 312.

38. Ibid., p. 205.

39. Alfred M. Lee, *The Daily Newspaper in America* (New York: Macmillan, 1937), p. 607.

40. Don Seitz, *The James Gordon Bennetts* (Indianapolis: Bobbs-Merrill, 1928), pp. 20–21.

41. [Isaac C. Pray], *Memoirs of James Gordon Bennett and His Times* (New York: Stringer and Townsend, 1855; Arno reprint ed., 1970), pp. 74–75.

42. Ibid., p. 117. See also Wallace B. Eberhard, "Mr. Bennett Covers a Murder Trial," *Journalism Quarterly* 47 (1970):457–63.

43. Seitz, p. 15.

44. Lee, p. 610.

45. Bleyer, p. 157.

46. [Thomas Gill], *Court Reports* (Boston: Otis, Broaders & Co., 1837), p. 104.

47. "Explosion Claims," *New York Evening Post*, 7 February 1902, p. 12.

48. *New York Evening Post*, 8 September 1852, p. 2.

49. "Funk in Jail," *Chicago Tribune*, 24 April 1885, p. 8.

50. Bleyer, p. 156.

51. Lee, p. 609.

52. Mott, p. 51.

53. Bleyer, p. 74.

54. Lee, p. 604.

55. Mott, p. 197.

56. Ibid., pp. 51, 101.

57. Michael Schudson, *Discovering the News* (New York: Basic Books, 1978), p. 22.

58. Lee, pp. 603–04.

59. Bleyer, pp. 157–58. Bleyer also concluded that the two most popular features of the penny press were humorous treatment of police court cases and reports of sensational murder trials. Ibid., p. 156.

60. Further evidence of this overstatement is provided by Kenneth D. Nordin, "The Entertaining Press: Sensationalism in Eighteenth Century Boston Newspapers," *Communication Research* 6 (July 1979):295–320. See also Susan M. Kingsbury et al., *Newspapers and the News,* (New York: G.P. Putnam's Sons, 1937), p. 169.

61. *Boston News-Letter*, 9–16 February 1719.

62. *New York Gazette*, 13–20 March 1727.

63. Ibid., 14–21 October 1734. The political overtones of such coverage are obvious, and publisher Bradford did allow his newspaper to be used by the administration. See, e.g., Emery, pp. 43–44.

64. *Boston Gazette*, 1–8 May 1721. The execution was noted by one sentence in the following week's paper.

65. For a representative example, see *Boston News-Letter*, 15–22 August 1734.

66. *Boston News-Letter*, 10–17 May 1733.

67. Ibid., 16–23 August 1733.

68. Ibid., 23–30 August 1733.

69. These conclusions will be bolstered by examples presented throughout this chapter.

70. *Boston Evening Post*, 6 March 1738.

71. See, e.g., "The First 'Struck' Jury," *New York Tribune*, 28 November 1872, p. 1.

72. More specific illustrations of the type of civil coverage appear throughout this chapter. Table 3.1, which shows the type of courts covered, also suggests the breadth of coverage civil actions received.

73. *Boston Gazette*, 5–12 December 1737.

74. Ibid., 6–13 April 1741.

75. *Boston Evening Post*, 28 September 1772.

76. "Meeting of the Bar," *New York Herald*, 2 October 1846, p. 2.

77. *New York Evening Post*, 13 May 1862, p. 3.

78. See, e.g., *New York Evening Post*, 21 February 1872, p. 1; "Charles O'Conor," *New York Herald*, 12 April 1876, p. 4; "O'Conor Vindicated," *New York Herald*, 1 June 1876, p. 5; "The Bar Association," *Chicago Tribune*, 7 March 1875, p. 15.

79. *Chicago Tribune*, 31 December 1875, p. 5.

80. *Philadelphia Public Ledger*, 13 June 1887, p. 4.

81. *New York Tribune*, 28 July 1842, p. 3.

82. *Philadelphia Public Ledger*, 18 July 1887, p. 3.

83. "An Offended Justice," *New York Tribune*, 18 July 1862, p. 2.

84. Ibid., 29 August 1872, p. 1. A reporter feigned insanity and was easily committed to an institution.

85. *New York Evening Post*, 6 May 1872, p. 3.

86. "Come to Judgment," *Chicago Tribune*, 20 January 1875, p. 7.

87. "Fees in District Court," *New York Herald*, 22 September 1886, p. 5.

88. "Our Taxes," *Chicago Tribune*, 7 August 1875, p. 2.

89. See appendix A for a representative sample.

90. *Boston News-Letter*, 15–22 August 1734.

91. Ibid., 16–23 September 1736.

92. See, e.g., *Boston News-Letter*, 9–16 February 1719; *New York Gazette*, 4–11 February 1735.

93. *Boston Evening Post*, 9 August 1773.

94. *New York Evening Post*, 13 May 1807.

95. Lee, p. 608.

96. Ibid.

97. Ibid., p. 611.

98. Seitz, pp. 20–21.

99. Joseph E. Chamberlin, *The Boston Transcript* (Boston: Houghton Mifflin, 1930), pp. 16–17. Bennett covered the same case. See Eberhard, pp. 457–63.

100. See, e.g., *New York Evening Post*, 10 January 1827, for such a credit line over a report from the court of sessions.

101. See, e.g., *Boston Transcript*, 15 December 1831, p. 2, for a similar credit line.

102. Emery, p. 120.

103. Bleyer, pp. 165–66.

104. James Parton, *The Life Horace Greeley* (New York: Mason Bros., 1855), p. 396.

105. Ibid.

106. Lee, p. 624. Lee also notes that shorthand reporters received the most pay, but frequently left journalism because they could make even more as legal reporters (for the courts). Ibid., p. 626.

107. "The Gambler's Victim," *Chicago Tribune*, 27 November 1875, p. 10.

108. "Alleged Police Outrage," *New York Evening Post*, 2 October 1882, p. 1.

109. "Still Under Lock and Key," *New York Herald*, 24 November 1886, p. 4.

110. "Mr. Woolsey's Surprise," *New York Tribune*, 23 November 1892, p. 7. The story begins: "Edward J. Woolsey came into the reporters' room at the County Court House yesterday."

111. *Boston News-Letter*, 7–14 August 1704.

112. *Boston Gazette*, 27 April–4 May 1724.

113. *Boston Evening Post*, 5 December 1774.

114. See, e.g., *Boston News-Letter*, 15–22 August 1734; and *Philadelphia Public Ledger*, 2 October 1877, p. 1. Countless additional examples could be cited.

115. "The Ring Criminals," *New York Tribune*, 8 February 1872, p. 1.

116. "Ties up the Trust," *Chicago Tribune*, 31 January 1895, p. 1.

117. "Local Politics," *Chicago Tribune*, 25 November 1885, p. 6.

118. *New York Evening Post*, 10 May 1872, p. 4.

119. "The Dutchess County Case," Ibid., 9 February 1892, p. 1.

120. "Proof Is Not Lacking," *Chicago Tribune*, 24 November 1895, p. 7.

121. "Witnesses Against W. H. Young," *New York Evening Post*, 25 September 1902, p. 1.

122. "The First 'Struck' Jury," *New York Tribune*, 28 November 1872, p. 1.

123. See, e.g., *Chicago Tribune*, 24 September 1875, p. 8; "Denouncing Her Betrayer in Court," *New York Tribune*, 11 November 1882, p. 8; "An Arrest for Forgerie," *Philadelphia Public Ledger*, 6 September 1887, p. 1.

124. See, e.g., "The Charge Against Leon Bernard," *New York Tribune*, 26 April 1882, p. 8. Here an attorney declined to comment "fearing that publicity would interfere with the proposed steps [in the case]."

125. "To Sue for $200,000," *New York Tribune*, 13 September 1902, p. 9.

126. Lee, p. 617.

127. "More About the French Frauds," *New York Herald*, 30 September 1856, p. 3.

128. "The Grand Jury in Court," *New York Tribune*, 12 February 1872, p. 1.

129. "The Accused Commissioners," *Chicago Tribune*, 26 June 1875, p. 8.

130. Ibid., 1 October 1875, p. 7.

131. "The Gambler's Victim," Ibid., 27 November 1875, p. 10.

132. "Schlesinger and Mayer," Ibid., 29 September 1885, p. 3.

133. "The M'Cunn Estate," *New York Herald*, 24 June 1876, p. 6.

134. "Have No Party Rights," *Philadelphia Public Ledger*, 9 February 1897, p. 1.

135. "The Jury," *New York Herald*, 9 June 1836, p. 1.

136. "Justice Humbugged," Ibid., 25 November 1886, p. 5.

137. "Juror Looked for Evidence," *New York Tribune*, 13 June 1902, p. 7. I assume the juror made his statement to the reporter.

138. Ibid., 12 February 1872, p. 1.

139. "To Probe It Alone," *Chicago Tribune*, 29 September 1895, p. 1.

140. *Philadelphia Public Ledger*, 11 May 1867, p. 1.

141. "Pleads Not Guilty," *New York Herald*, 13 September 1895, p. 6.

142. "Was Another's Wife," Ibid., 29 September 1895, p. 5.

143. "The Greenpoint Tragedy," Ibid., 31 January 1876, p. 3.

144. "The Prisoner," *Chicago Tribune*, 27 November 1875, p. 10.

145. *Boston News-Letter*, 30 June–7 July 1726.

146. *New York Gazette*, 21–28 January 1733.

147. *Boston News-Letter*, 9–16 February 1719.

148. *Boston Evening Post*, 8 September 1755.

149. *Philadelphia Aurora*, 8 May 1801.

150. Ibid., 14 May 1801.

151. I have noted above how reporters frequently interviewed sources on both sides of legal disputes.

152. *New York Evening Post*, 26 April 1842, p. 2. The story concluded by noting a verdict for the plaintiff and giving the names of the attorneys.

153. *New York Tribune*, 19 July 1842, p. 3.

154. *Philadelphia Public Ledger*, 24 June 1867, p. 1.

155. *New York Tribune*, 8 June 1842, p. 1.

156. Ibid., 9–14 June 1842.

157. At least one commentator, however, has argued that police court reporting had a positive impact. "These early police reporters created models for varied literary treatment of formal courtroom sources; their freedom in reporting speech

as dialect, in characterizing participants in news events, and in transforming testimony from question-answer interrogation into narrative scenes expanded the boundaries for future exposures. They supplied some of the raw ingredients for muckraking, and, most important, they advanced awareness that reporters would find their stylistic heritage in literature—not in the business ledger or the legal brief." Warren Francke, "Sensational Roots: The Police Court Heritage," University of Nebraska at Omaha (undated) (mimeographed), p. 21.

158. Gill, p. 37. Such items also raise a question about the audience to which reporters were addressing themselves. Certainly, this language—and that in a great number of other court stories—is sophisticated and would require a highly literate reader. Was this writing really aimed at a mass of newly literate Americans? Yet such is the most generally accepted view. See, e.g., Emery, p. 119.

159. *Boston Transcript*, 10 May 1841, p. 2.

160. "An Impudent Swindle," *Chicago Tribune*, 25 April 1855, p. 3.

161. *New York Tribune*, 22 June 1872, p. 2.

162. "H. L. Durrie Charged with Grand Larceny," Ibid., 31 May 1892, p. 12.

163. "The Webster Jury Out," Ibid., 5 March 1892, p. 2.

164. "E. M. Field's Trial," *New York Evening Post*, 23 February 1892, p. 11.

165. At least two murder trials were interrupted because of disorderly crowds. See Emery, p. 123; and the *Boston Transcript*, 31 March 1850, p. 1. In at least two others, police were either worried about imminent disorder or had trouble keeping order. See *New York Evening Post*, 12 February 1872, p. 3; and *New York Herald*, 19 January 1866, p. 2.

166. *New York Evening Post*, 6 June 1828, quoting from *New York Statesman*, 5 June 1828, cited by Bleyer, p. 157.

167. Bleyer, p. 172.

168. *Boston Transcript*, 6 June 1836, cited by Bleyer, p. 150.

169. *New York Tribune*, 19 April 1841, cited by Bleyer, p. 215.

170. See, e.g., Emery, p. 125.

171. Bleyer, p. 166.

172. Ibid., p. 173.

173. Lambert A. Wilmer, *Our Press Gang* (Philadelphia: Lloyd, 1859; Arno reprint ed., 1970), p. 52.

174. Ibid., p. 228.

175. Ibid., p. 230.

176. Gay Talese, *The Kingdom and the Power* (New York: Bantam, 1970), pp. 109–10.

177. "Miss Gannon Arrested," *New York Herald*, 29 September 1886, p. 5.

178. Ibid.

179. "Trial by Newspaper," *Albany Law Journal* 11 (1875):248.

180. Ibid., p. 249.

181. Ibid.

182. "Newspaper Reports of Legal Proceedings," *Central Law Journal* 3 (1876):524.

183. "Trial by Newspaper," *American Law Review* 18 (1884):1038.

184. William S. Forrest, "Trial by Newspapers," *Criminal Law Magazine* 14 (1892):553.

185. David Rothman, *The Discovery of the Asylum* (Boston: Little, Brown & Co., 1971), p. xix.

186. Friedman, p. 63.

187. Richard M. Brown, "Historical Patterns of Violence in America," in *Violence in America: Historical and Comparative Perspectives* (Washington, D.C.: U.S. Government Printing Office, 1969), pp. 40–41.

188. Ibid., p. 45.

189. Friedman, p. 521.

190. Ibid., p. 504.

191. Ibid., p. 253; see generally, John P. Roche, "American Liberty: An Examination of the Tradition of Freedom," in John P. Roche, *Shadow and Substance: Essays on the Theory and Structure of Politics* (New York: Macmillan, 1964), pp. 3–38.

192. Brown, p. 51. According to Brown, Teddy Roosevelt, as a young North Dakota cattle rancher, begged to be admitted to a vigilante band fighting rustlers and horse thieves, but he was rebuffed.

193. Rothman, p. 245.

194. Hughes, pp. 157–58.

195. Friedman, p. 266.

196. Ibid., p. 277.

197. Ibid., p. 266.

198. Alfred Z. Reed, *Training for the Public Profession of the Law* (Boston: Merrymount, 1921), p. 79.

199. Friedman, p. 276.

200. Ibid., p. 270.

201. Ibid., p. 273. The *New York Tribune* actually reported an instance of an attorney attempting to bribe its reporter to publish a full account of a case. "Elias's Tricks," *New York Tribune*, 9 March 1872, p. 8.

202. Friedman, p. 273.

203. Gerhard O. W. Mueller, "Problems Posed by Publicity to Crime and Criminal Proceedings," *University of Pennsylvania Law Review* 110 (1961):6.

204. Friedman, p. 275.

205. Reed, p. 206.

206. Ibid., p. 224, n. 1. Alabama was the first state to have a code.

207. Clearly there were cases involving contempt by publication of information about the judiciary that predate 1830, but those cases involved an additional element—criticism of a judge or court. For example, the case of Respublica v. Oswald, 1 Dallas 319 (Pa. 1788), which led Pennsylvania ultimately to adopt legislation controlling the contempt power, involved a man who wrote that he was afraid of a state court justice whom he thought would be prejudiced against him.

208. Trial of John Francis Knapp, 7 Am. State Trials 395, 411 (Mass. 1830).

209. Eberhard, p. 461. After founding the *New York Herald*, Bennett had a similar encounter with another judge. *New York Herald*, 12 March 1836, p. 1.

210. Eberhard, p. 461.

211. Pa. Acts 1808–1809, ch. 78, p. 146. See also, "Contempt by Publication," *Northwestern University Law Review* 60 (1965):540–41.

212. N.Y Rev. Stat. 1829, Part iii, ch. iii, tit. 2, art. 1 § 10. See also Walter Nelles and Carol Weiss King, "Contempt by Publication in the United States," *Columbia Law Review* 28 (1928):401–31.

213. 4 Stat. 487 (1831). For a comparison of the Pennsylvania, New York and federal statutes, see Nelles and King, pp. 528–29.

214. Ronald L. Goldfarb. *The Contempt Power* (Garden City, N.Y.: Anchor, 1971), p. 19.

215. United States v. Holmes, 26 Fed. Cas. 360, 363 (C.C.E.D. Pa. 1842).

216. Ibid.

217. John Lofton, *Justice and the Press* (Boston: Beacon, 1966), p. 115. Lofton provides no citation for the case.

218. "Trial of the Rioters," *Chicago Tribune* 19 June 1855, p. 3.

219. Ibid.

220. The *New York Herald*, 16 October 1846, p. 1, reprinted an item from a Richmond newspaper noting that defense counsel in a murder case there had "intended" to seek a court order suppressing ex parte statements, but did not follow through. The *Chicago Tribune*, 8 August 1875, p. 16, reported that the prosecutor in a forgery case "remarked to the Court that he should have that paper [one of the *Tribune's* competitors] attached for contempt" for speculating on the verdict. There is no evidence that the matter was pursued.

221. The record is virtually bare of reported cases in which newspapers were punished for publishing material obtained in open court. It is true that from the Civil War until World War I, state and federal courts abrogated contempt statutes and returned to the English common-law rules which gave them sweeping power. Donald M. Gillmor and Jerome A. Barron, *Mass Communication Law*, 2d ed., (St. Paul: West, 1974), p. 470. Again, however, the publications that caused problems were those critical of the judiciary. Nelles and King's survey of all reported contempt by publication cases after 1831 confirms this. Nelles and King, pp. 554–62. The only exceptions are Telegram Newspaper Co. v. Commonwealth, 172 Mass. 294, 52 N.E. 445 (1899); and *in re* Shortridge, 99 Cal. 256, 34 P. 227 (1893). In Telegram Newspaper, a newspaper was fined $100 for publishing extrajudicial information about a pending civil action which the court found to be calculated to obstruct justice. But in Shortridge, a state supreme court reversed a $100 contempt fine against a newspaper that had defied a court order and printed testimony in a divorce case from which public and press had been barred.

222. See n. 221.

223. Harold L. Nelson, *Libel in News of Congressional Investigating Committees* (Minneapolis: University of Minnesota Press, 1961), pp. 10–11. Nelson reports that a long search turned up only two libel cases stemming from newspaper reports of judicial proceedings. The newspaper won one of the cases; the other involved editorial comment mixed with a story. Ibid., p. 147, n. 29. Nelson's conclusion squares with Hudson's contemporary history. See n. 224 below.

224. Frederic Hudson, *Journalism in the United States* (New York: Haskell House, 1873; reprint ed., 1968), p. 478.

225. Ibid.

226. N.Y. Laws 1854, chap. 130.

227. Nelson, p. 8.

228. Kathryn Dix Sowle, "Defamation and the First Amendment: The Case for a Constitutional Privilege of Fair Report," *New York University Law Review* 54 (1979): 478.

229. Ibid., p. 476. See also, Nelson, p. 12.

230. Cowley v. Pulsifer, 137 Mass. 392 (1884). See also Nelson, pp. 7–8.

231. Hudson, p. 747. Citing a *New York Herald* story, Hudson reports that in

1869 when his book was published, 756 libel suits were pending against U.S. newspapers for damages totaling $47.5 million.

232. Edwin L. Shuman, *Practical Journalism* (New York: D. Appleton & Co., 1903), p. 242.

233. Schudson, p. 6.

234. Ibid., p. 7.

235. Ibid., pp. 78–79.

236. Ibid., p. 71.

237. See text, p. 62.

238. See text, p. 50.

239. Judges might have been sources without any acknowledgment in stories, but there is no way to know. Of course, judges may have desired publicity because of political ambitions. To some degree, the desired visibility may have been an inherent by-product of verbatim reporting; but if political ambition were a major motivation, one would expect to see judges as more frequent and cooperative sources.

240. See text, p. 50.

241. Again, the terms are Nimmo's.

4

A Case Study in Judicial Reporting

This chapter presents an observational case study of one full-time court reporter for a daily newspaper in Minnesota. Although it has the drawbacks of any observational study—most notably lack of generalizability—this approach has the strength of allowing the researcher to observe the news-gathering process firsthand, to study not merely what reporters and sources say but what they do. Observation is particularly suited to relationships among several persons considered simultaneously and thus relevant to the news-gathering process.[1] It provides access to data not accessible in any other way and provides richness as a supplement to the survey data presented later. In the following pages, I describe the method used in this observational study, present my observations and discuss them.

METHOD

I spent four days following and observing a full-time court reporter for a metropolitan daily newspaper in Minnesota during July 1979. The reporter—for whom I will use the pseudonym "Bill"—agreed to being observed after I generally explained the nature of my research. His immediate editors also agreed.

Bill has a bachelor's degree in journalism and, at the time of the study, had been a newspaper reporter for eight years, although he had had two leaves of absence. He used one leave to work for a pretrial diversion program and another for a fellowship to study law and history at a major university. He has progressed from general assignment reporter to police reporter to court reporter. He has covered courts for four years.

The beat he covers is immense. It includes thirty-six state and local judges and their staffs; seventy-two attorneys in the county attorney's office and twenty in the city attorney's office; fifty public defenders; about twenty private criminal defense attorneys; fifteen private attorneys; court administration staff; the U.S. attorney's office (twelve prosecutors); four federal judges and their staffs; three federal magistrates; bankruptcy court; the FBI; the Drug Enforcement Administration; the Secret Service; clerks in federal law enforcement and judicial offices; bar associations; the Minnesota Supreme Court (although he generally relies on AP coverage of it); the state Lawyers Professional Responsibility Board; and the state Board on Judicial Standards.

On Bill's desk are a dictionary, a small law dictionary, a text on media law, a copy of the federal rules of criminal procedure, telephone books, notebooks, piles of newspapers, and books on crime victims, the rights of young people, and grand juries. His working hours are generally 9:30 A.M. to 6:30 P.M.

Bill agreed to let me follow him everywhere with the understanding that at the first indication that my presence might be interfering with his contact with sources, I would give him privacy. Bill would introduce me to his sources to explain briefly my presence; he generally gave my name and indicated that I was conducting research. But very few sources asked who I was; frequently I was ignored; and Bill never asked me to leave while he talked to a source. In fact, Bill said he perceived no effect on his sources from my presence. Of course, there is no way I can know whether my presence affected Bill. I can only say that there was no facially obvious indication of an effect.

I tried to be as unobtrusive as possible. I made notes only when I had an opportunity to be alone several times during the day.

The only times my presence was clearly recognized by Bill's sources came when one or two sources expressed interest in my research and when I was used as fodder for sources who teased Bill. For example, some attorneys asked why I had chosen not to watch a "real" newspaper reporter or why I had chosen to watch someone working for a "student" newspaper. Since I did observe Bill in the newsroom, as well as on the beat, I was noticed by other reporters and editors. Initially, some of them teased Bill for at last having his own writing coach or referred to me as "the shadow." But even such notice lasted only a day.

The only occasions on which I did more than quietly observe were when I privately asked Bill about some of his attitudes about his work.

OBSERVATIONS

Day 1

Bill goes directly from the office to a county commissioner who has written a memo suggesting budget cuts in a unit of the county attorney's office that is prosecuting her husband. The story has originated with a tip from someone in the county attorney's office several weeks ago, and the memo has subsequently been obtained and passed on to Bill by a fellow reporter. But Bill is unhappy because a broadcast reporter has scooped him by breaking the story yesterday. Bill interviews the commissioner for a half-hour and is on a first-name basis with her. She complains that no reporter has been in the county commissioner's meeting room yet this summer, and Bill agrees.

Bill next goes to the county budget director to see whether there have been similar memos from other commissioners. Then he attempts unsuccessfully to reach the county attorney for comment.

Bill has another potentially useful tip, this one regarding allegedly sexist comments made by a district judge in court to a black female attorney. The tip has come from "someone in the [courthouse] building." But Bill is unsuccessful in trying to contact the attorney, so he heads for municipal court to glance at its calendar and then for district court to check criminal complaints and search warrants. There a clerk kids him that an order has been filed ordering that all newspaper reporters are to be shot.

As he heads for the civil division, Bill meets a judge in the hall, chats briefly about judicial appointments and engages in some good-natured banter. Then he moves on to the civil division where he checks with a clerk on whom he relies for tips on interesting new cases. The clerk tells him there is nothing. Bill tells me later that this clerk has never let him down, and even if he had, Bill couldn't complain because the clerk helps as a favor that saves Bill from looking through perhaps thirty cases a day.

Back in his courthouse office, Bill again tries unsuccessfully to reach the attorney to whom the judge had made allegedly sexist comments. With that, Bill heads for lunch with an attorney friend. The attorney is really more friend than source. There is some discussion about which prosecuting attorneys are the best, but primarily lunch talk is small talk.

Bill heads for the federal building. He greets the district court clerks by first name, and they tip him about a products liability case and the sentencing of a fugitive bank robber. The federal judges are not available. A brief stop at the U.S. marshal's office produces another tip on a robbery sentencing, and Bill tells the source that a defendant in another case has now appeared before a federal magistrate in another town. That interests the source, but later Bill explains to me that although sources frequently ask him for information, he will not accommodate them except for information which is already on the public record or which has been published.

Bill's next stop is the office of the U.S. attorney. There he chats with several assistant U.S. attorneys about two other cases. The talk is friendly but not particularly substantive. In fact, Bill tells me later, attorneys seldom provide new information, but they may confirm and react. He says he believes attorneys like to see their names in print—for ego satisfaction, for advertising value and to influence cases. He finds criminal defense attorneys to be the most cooperative, prosecutors the least cooperative. And he believes attorneys and judges read his stories closely and carefully, often to see how he has handled things they may be familiar with and to learn what their colleagues are doing. At the same time, Bill says he worries that sources often don't understand that he is writing for a lay audience, not for specialists. He also thinks that after too long on the beat, a reporter either hates all his sources or becomes one of them, writing for them.

Back at the county courthouse, Bill calls on a judge, apparently looking for help in tracking down the sexist comment story. But the judge hides behind a newspaper, and Bill leaves. Later he tells me, "the more they [sources] refuse to cooperate, the more I want to write the story." And he does want the sexist comment story, but source after source leads only to dead ends. Finally, he locates an attorney who knows the "victim" well, but the source simply walks away from Bill. Bill follows. The source walks faster and literally turns his back to all questions. Bill is disgusted but gives up; he is surprised because that has never happened to him before.

Bill heads back to his courthouse office and meets a judge in the elevator. "You have a tough job," the judge tells him. "I always like to have you come by."

By telephone, Bill reaches the county attorney to obtain his reaction to the commissioner's memo with which he began the day. It is now 3:15. Bill tells the county attorney what the commissioner has told him and sounds somewhat incredulous himself. The county attorney does want to respond. He gives Bill some information apparently off the record, and Bill urges him to allow him to use it. Later Bill notes that he strictly honors good sources' requests for "off the record." In fact, he occasionally initiated off-the-record exchanges himself by prefacing questions with "just between you and me" or "any way to use this without connecting it to you?"

Before leaving for the newspaper office, Bill contacts a judge by telephone to obtain factual information on a murder defendant's acquittal. The judge has forgotten who Bill is.

It is 3:30 when Bill returns to the newspaper office and tells his editors what he has. He is frustrated when he discovers that only five minutes before he arrived, the victim of the judge's allegedly sexist remarks has called. He has given up on trying to write that story until tomorrow. Meanwhile, an attorney calls to say that the state will appeal a decision striking down part of the state's abortion-funding law, and Bill contacts another source for detail on the county commissioner story. Then, at 4:20, he reaches the attorney whose call he had missed an hour earlier. She is reluctant, and Bill tries to convince her to cooperate. He lays out his rationale for wanting to do the story and says he realizes that there is a legitimate balance between the importance of the story and the potential embarrassment to her. Finally, she agrees to provide the statement made to her by the judge, but she will not comment on the statement.

When Bill hangs up, he reads the judge's remark to several nearby reporters. They agree it may have been racist, sexist at least, and that it was ridiculous.

At 4:50 P.M., Bill begins to write his first story, the county commissioner story. He struggles with the lead sentence, then decides he needs to go for a walk and a Coke before finishing. He worries that there is really nothing hard and solid in the story as he finishes it just before 6 P.M., but the story runs on the front of the second section. Finally he writes a story on the abortion case appeal. It takes 20 minutes. Then he finishes the murder acquittal story.

Bill knows that tomorrow he will have the story on the judge's indiscreet comments.

Day 2

Bill arrives at the newspaper office, examines his mail and heads for coffee with two other reporters. They talk shop and then share a blatantly sexist joke just before discussing Bill's pending story on the judge's sexist comments. They apparently recognize something of a double standard at work but note that the judge is a public figure.

Bill returns to his desk, checks for messages and notes, and heads for the courthouse. There, his first action is to call the reporter—also a friend— who scooped him on the county commissioner story. He tells me he respects this reporter. They discuss the story, and Bill heads for arraignment court, but he stays for less than five minutes. Bill says he often chats with attorneys there about potentially newsworthy cases they might know about. But today he talks to no one.

Now Bill must approach the judge who made the allegedly sexist comments. The judge, ironically, notes that he believes Bill's story was pretty tough on the county commissioner. Then Bill eases into his reason for coming to the judge; the judge is very cooperative. Bill continues to assure him that he is not doing a story for personal reasons but because this story must be told. "I don't blame you," the judge replies. He shows Bill a copy of the letter of complaint he received from the attorney, and a quotation, counseling more discretion, which he is taping to his bench. Bill's approach throughout is low key; he says he prefers to be that way and would be aggressive only if a source were uncooperative. He is also impressed with the forthright manner in which the judge handled the situation. "I would have been hard-ass," he tells me. "But . . . . This is when it's hard. I like him." Several times he mentions to other sources and colleagues that he is not trying to do a "gonzo job" on the judge, although he seems clearly to relish the story.

Bill returns briefly to his courthouse office to fill in detail in his notes before he forgets, then heads for the office of another judge who is apparently a good source to explain the outcome of the story and for a bit of gossip. The judge is interested, but also ventilates—partly to me, I suspect—about the sins of the local press. Later, Bill admits that he may be too close to that judge and that "I guess I haven't written anything really negative about him."

As Bill returns to his office, he meets another judge in the elevator and tells her that he has quite a story in the offing about one of her colleagues; he also asks her about a case she has under advisement. Bill leaves the elevator and walks toward the office. He probably would write a less fair story, he concedes, had the judge been really uncooperative.

Just before lunch, Bill receives a tip from a source in a federal law enforcement agency that charges have been filed against four persons for blowing up telephone booths. After lunch, he visits the agency, and an agent reads information to him from his records. On the wall, a previous newspaper story about an agency case is posted. As he leaves, Bill tells an agent that he recalls owing him a beer. Bill had, however, had to ask quite a few questions even to get all the factual specifics from the agents.

Bill goes to the federal clerks to obtain a copy of the criminal complaint filed in the case and, while there, meets a federal magistrate who teasingly complains about lack of contact with Bill. Bill follows the magistrate back to his office, and they chat about a highly publicized federal court case, speculate on the sentence the defendants in it are likely to receive and discuss the incident that led to the case. Then Bill returns to the clerks' office to check on civil actions. He greets the clerks and heads to the federal prosecutors' offices.

Bill seeks more detail about a criminal case from one of the prosecutors, but the prosecutor is very uncertain about how much he can safely say. A second prosecutor enters the office and kiddingly remarks about his own desire for publicity in a recent case. "I certainly never expected the cameras when I came out of court with my prepared statement," he jokes. Then the two prosecutors seriously complain to Bill about coverage by another reporter of the resignation of their boss. Bill neither agrees nor disagrees but later remarks that he believes the criticism was unfounded. He says he believes he is adept at handling such source ventilations.

Bill returns to the county courthouse to see a copy of the judge's apology letter [in the sexist remark incident], then makes a quick stop to check district court records. While he is checking search warrants, Bill is approached by a law clerk who tips him that a judge has filed an order compelling the county to give a hearing to two interns it fired. Bill asks a civil court clerk whether there is "anything new," then obtains a copy of the order from the judge's clerk. As Bill is copying the order, another judge stops to tell him about a criminal sexual conduct trial and conviction in his court. The case is newsworthy, he believes, because it is rather gruesome and because the defendant had just been paroled on virtually the same charge. He shows Bill the file; but Bill does not commit himself. Later, Bill notes that he will not often do a small story just to please a source.

Bill phones the newspaper office with his "budget" of stories for the day and at 3:45 returns to the office himself. He telephones for the ages and addresses of the explosion defendants, then obtains a file on the intern-firing incident from another reporter. Amid telephone calls, at 4 P.M. he begins the story on the judge's indiscreet comments. Later, he says he believes he could come up with numerous additional stories but is limited because he is compelled by editors to return to the newsroom about 3:30 every day.

Day 3

Bill doesn't work during the morning because of a dental appointment, but by 1:30 P.M. he is in the newspaper office complaining to an assistant city editor that a copy editor had changed the meaning of part of his story on the judge's allegedly sexist remarks. The editor had removed the designation of the attorney as "black" from Bill's lead, changed "shoestring budget" to "small budget" and changed "perennially" to "often." Then Bill scans the newly decided state supreme court cases but decides to leave coverage to the Associated Press. He writes a quick summary of a combination interview–book review on which he is working and heads for the county courthouse.

Bill must work fast this afternoon. He goes directly to the district court clerks and there meets a bail bondsman he knows. He suggests that Bill had written a tough story on the judge but compliments him for being honest and true to his word. They speculate on the outcome of a highly publicized out-of-town murder trial.

The bondsman leaves and Bill briefly teases a clerk. She replies that she'll no longer offer him anything and he'll just have to dig stories out on his own. Bill checks with the civil court clerk for new cases but the clerk says there is nothing. Bill checks for new documents but finds nothing. He kids the clerks on his way out.

At the county attorney's offfice, Bill picks up the office's daily diary. He begins trading good-natured insults with several assistant county attorneys. They discuss a betting pool on the time and verdict in an out-of-town murder case. The attorneys call Bill by their own nickname. Bill notes that the attorneys seem to have been losing a few cases lately, but he also asks an attorney when his and his wife's baby is due. One attorney complains that Bill's story on the judge's indiscreet comments was too soft on the judge, but generally the attorneys liked the story and agreed with the need to publish it. Finally, a receptionist begs for quiet, and Bill tells her that the best information comes from her anyway. One attorney complains that another reporter had been biased in covering a trial a year earlier and that he had eaten out of the defense's hand. Bill listens.

A check on a source in the city attorney's office is unsuccessful. The source is out. So Bill heads for municipal court to chat with a juvenile judge, but he is in a hearing so Bill small talks with the bailiff who immediately mentions the story on the judge's comments and is not critical of it. Bill explains his position on the story—namely, that it was a foolish remark for a district judge to have made.

Bill heads for the federal building and in the court clerks' office finds an order that might interest another reporter.[2] He phones him and photocopies the order. His interest is aroused by another order, this one in a police harassment case. He asks a clerk what it's about, decides to call the attorneys involved, but notes the award is small and the case is four years old. Another clerk says she has read his story on the judge. Bill asks whether a federal judge has read it; the clerks think he has but are not certain.

Bill checks the U.S. magistrate's office and the federal prosecutors' office, but no one is at either office. He returns to the newspaper office for coffee with other reporters. The discussion is basically office talk, but Bill seems pleased that the other reporters liked his story on the judge.

Back at his desk, Bill spends the rest of his workday writing a feature interview he had done several days earlier with the authors of a book. It has been a quiet news day.

Day 4

Bill begins the day in another city in federal court to cover the sentencing of several men in a highly publicized criminal case. As he enters the courtroom, Bill is greeted by name by one of the defendants, and he nods in return. The sentences are announced; Bill murmurs "Jesus!" because he is so surprised at the length of the prison terms. He seems immediately to seize on that as the angle for his story, and when court adjourns, he expresses his shock to the defense attorneys. Meanwhile, the judge's law clerk hands Bill and other reporters copies of the judge's statement to the defendants. Bill is primarily interested in obtaining reactions to the sentences. The defense attorneys indicate that they, too, expected lesser sentences.

Later, in a courthouse hallway, Bill notes to an attorney that one of the defendants even thanked the judge. Another attorney says "[one defendant] is crazy, but that's off the record." Bill seems to agree with that assessment, and he remarks on it several times, but not in his story. The attorneys' comments, however, are generally vague. Upon Bill's request, one of them does, however, give Bill the name of a case the same judge heard five years earlier involving some of the same people who were indirectly involved in the criminal cases just decided. Later, Bill obtains the file on that case in the federal clerks' office. He first plans to use the information in his story since it vaguely suggests that the judge might have been less than objective. He includes the information in his first draft of the story and shows it to other reporters in the newsroom. They worry that it appears loaded against the judge, too far removed from the main story and out of context. Bill agrees and removes the information.

Bill also interviews one defendant's spouse in the hallway outside the courtroom. A crowd gathers around during the interview, and Bill conducts the interview much more formally than his interviews with the attorneys. The interview ends and Bill wishes her good luck. Bill telephones his editors to tell them what has happened and heads back to the office. It is late morning now. Bill discusses the events with other reporters. "He's [one of the defendants] crazy," he notes to one reporter, "but Jesus Christ that's a lot of [prison] time." Then it is time for lunch.

After lunch, Bill heads for the county courthouse and the chambers of a judge who has a tip on a campaign law case he is to hear. He shows Bill the complaint and jokes that he'll have to rule in favor of the plaintiff "since your precious First Amendment is at stake, although Justice Burger would disapprove." He kids a bit more, then promises to give Bill the scoop when he decides the case. The judge also complains about another reporter who, he claims, interfered with a grand jury investigation. Later, Bill says he believes it was a judge who leaked that information about the grand jury. But Bill also wonders aloud how he could have missed the campaign law case when it was filed about a week ago.

Bill heads for the office of another judge, one he has visited several times in the past three days. He asks the judge what scuttlebutt he has heard in the wake of the story about the allegedly sexist comments. The judge says he has heard none, but he wonders what Bill has done with a tip he provided a day or two ago. Bill hedges, says he's been just too busy, says perhaps he'll pick up the story at sentencing.

The judge complains, partly to me, that the newspapers have been ridiculously boosting a couple of prominent criminal defense attorneys and that reporters like lawyers who do things like setting up free bars. Bill generally agrees. The judge teasingly suggests that Bill might actually sit in a courtroom sometime since he is a court reporter.[3]

Bill heads for the office of an assistant county attorney to chat and to see whether the attorney has heard any reaction to Bill's story on the county commissioner's memo. The attorney offers an unexpected tip about an accountant being charged with swindling an employer out of $700,000. A competing newspaper has already published the story, and again Bill wonders how he could have missed it. He goes to another attorney close to the case, obtains a copy of the complaint and urges the attorney to contact him with such material in the future. Bill also learns that the accountant has more or less admitted everything.

Bill is ready to walk to the federal building, but it is pouring rain so he heads back to his county courthouse office. He decides to make his federal rounds by telephone, and his first call is to the attorney who prosecuted the defendants sentenced this morning. Bill wants to know whether he, too, was surprised by the length of the sentences; he also asks for information on a further investigation and on the prior record of one of the defendants. It is not unusual for Bill to ask questions prefaced by "just between you and me." He contacts another federal prosecutor who has just returned from a vacation. They chat at length about the man's vacation; Bill asks about the man's wife and says it's good to have him back.

Back at the newspaper office, Bill gives the information on the campaign law case to a city government reporter, and that reporter writes the story. Bill writes his story on the criminal sentencing. He does not write a story on the alleged swindler.

Stories Written

In four days, then, Bill produced eight pieces of copy, including the feature interview with the authors of the book. Five were spot news stories related to cases: one on the appeal of the abortion law decision; one on the order requiring hearings for the fired county interns; one on the murder defendant's acquittal; one on the charges of bombing telephone booths; and one on the criminal case sentencings. The two other stories were pieces on the county commissioner's memo and the judge's indiscreet remarks. Bill had actually been in courtrooms only twice—arraignment court for several minutes and federal court for the sentencings.

Three of the stories were played either on the front page or on the first page of the second section.

DISCUSSION

General Observations

Bill seemed to prefer criminal coverage to civil coverage, although while I watched him, two of the five stories he wrote on cases were stories on civil actions. Both civil actions had political or constitutional implications. The feature interview aside, both noncase stories were either directly or indirectly related to criminal law: the commissioner's memo story because it was related to the state's prosecution of the commissioner's husband,

and the judge's remark story because it involved remarks made to an attorney during a criminal case, although that probably had no effect on the story's newsworthiness. This perceived preference for criminal coverage is also reflected in Bill's beat itself. The only attention specifically to civil cases came when he checked with the district court clerk who tipped him to such cases and when he checked records, generally in federal court. These checks, however, produced neither of the civil action stories Bill wrote. Both came from tips—one from an attorney by telephone and the other from a law clerk. And while Bill actually scanned some criminal complaints and search warrants in state district court, he simply asked the civil clerk whether there was "anything."

In a larger sense, it is striking how little of the tremendous volume of court activity Bill actually attended to and reported. For example, during one day of my observation, the state district court criminal calendar indicated the following activity: six felony trials on charges ranging from forgery to arson; ten arraignments on felony charges ranging from drug possession to wrongfully obtaining public assistance; three sentencings; twenty-four appearances, pleas or other dispositions in cases ranging from murder to swindling; and eight cases involving revocation of probation or parole, including persons initially charged with offenses ranging from drug dealing to robbery. The special term calendar for the day showed nontrial action scheduled on eighteen civil cases, not to mention case filings and civil trials. At the very least, then, action was scheduled in sixty-nine cases. Yet Bill wrote no spot news stories that day.

My observation suggests that what is covered is surprisingly chancy and related to factors in addition to the relative newsworthiness of the items which are and are not reported.[4] For example, Bill is clearly affected by time. He has only four to five hours a day in which to actually cover his huge beat. If he arrives at the county courthouse at 10 A.M. and contacts sources until noon and then breaks for lunch, he has only another two to three hours in the afternoon before he must return to the newspaper office, tell his editors what he has and begin to write. Bill is openly concerned about this constraint, which is to some degree imposed on him by his editors. How can one person efficiently deal with so many sources and so much information?

Perhaps this explains why Bill is actually in the courtroom so seldom. Direct observation can be costly in terms of time; to be worth Bill's investment, the information gained from direct observation must be extremely valuable, and consequently he must be extremely selective. He is almost forced to rely more on personal contact (i.e., interviewing and informal discussion) and documents. Thus his relationship with sources is crucial, not only for information but for help in determining where he should expend his time. This may add to sources' power and diminish Bill's.

Just how important good sources are to Bill is reflected by the fact that of the seven stories he wrote from information gathered while I was with him, no less than five resulted from tips. And he received several more tips while I observed him, some of which he ignored but at least one of which he passed on to another reporter who subsequently wrote a story. Of course, such reliance on sources can cut two ways. Bill was also somewhat disconcerted on two occasions when tips made him realize that he had missed interesting items that he felt he ought to have found on his own. The campaign law case had been filed for several days before the judge tipped Bill to it, and the swindle case—which Bill never did publish—should also have appeared in criminal court records. Obviously, there is no way of telling how many other stories may be missed.

Of course, Bill was not totally at the mercy of sources. As he glanced through court calendars and documents, he could look for newsworthy names and/or significant or unusual facts. He could also get an indication of where to invest his time based on what had been covered before, and in fact this indicator seemed to be at work in five of the seven stories I watched him write. The county commissioner's memo was newsworthy because the investigation of her husband had been a major story before. The criminal sentencings could be traced back to a highly publicized incident. The murder acquittal involved a case affected by a strike of state crime lab workers. The order requiring hearings for the fired interns followed their well-publicized firing. And the announcement of the appeal of the abortion law case came not only after the trial in that case but involved a highly publicized political issue. Nevertheless, Bill was tipped to three of these five.

The apparent importance of Bill's sources may contribute to his devotion to objectivity. Bill indicated constant concern about appearing objective. Although he may have let some of his sources know his subjective feelings, he was acutely careful not to let this happen in his stories. Sometimes his concern with objectivity spilled over from his conversations with sources into conversations with colleagues in the newsroom. This concern was especially evident when Bill did his story on the judge's indiscreet comments. He explained to source after source—and particularly to his more reluctant sources—how he had almost no choice but to do the story since it involved a significant indiscretion by a public official who is accountable to the public, and how he wanted to do a fair story and not a "gonzo job." He mentioned the same thing several times to other reporters, and he appeared very concerned about sources' reactions and reporters' reactions once the story was published. This same concern about the appearance of objectivity led him to remove some related information from the criminal sentencing story.

On one occasion, Bill noted to me that he couldn't afford to alienate too many sources or too many doors would be closed. Objectivity and overtly dissociating himself from stories may have been his primary shield against such an eventuality.

Exchange Behavior

Exchange behavior clearly occurred as Bill and his sources interacted, although they may not have consciously regarded it as such. If they were conscious of it, it was at the most general level. For example, Bill once remarked that a judge who had been cooperative probably liked publicity. And one prosecutor once jokingly noted that during a case he had never expected the TV cameras when he emerged with his prepared statement. Certainly, publicity and information are valuable commodities to trade, but this observational study suggests that they must be precisely defined and that other commodities also played important roles.

Consider first what sources could offer Bill. One thing is merely the enjoyment of the contact. And to a certain point, Bill did seem to enjoy the small talk and kidding that were part of his contact with many sources. Certainly a constantly tense and highly formal atmosphere would have made his job not only more difficult but much more unpleasant.

Sources could also offer Bill access to people, offices and perhaps even documents that would simply not be available to a person acting in another role. At first, it might seem that this special access is really unnecessary to Bill since so much of what the courts do is open to the public anyway. But, as already noted, Bill relied quite heavily on tips and information from personal sources. One of his most important stories—that on the judge's indiscreet comments—would have been virtually impossible without cooperation from sources. Without the tip, he might never have known about the incident, and without cooperation from the victim, he may never have obtained confirmation of the offending remark. Bill was allowed by court personnel to walk freely behind public counters, help himself to files and visit offices unannounced. Without such convenient access—particularly given his time constraints—Bill's job would have been much more difficult.

But the most important thing sources provided was information. This fell into several categories. First, there was straight factual information. This, in turn, might be either directly attributable, quotable information or it might be unquotable and/or unattributable information; it might be information central to the story or information primarily for background understanding. Sources offered Bill all these types of information as I watched, and often both parties understood implicitly which type of information was involved. Thus when one source told Bill that a defendant had admitted his offenses or when another referred to a defendant as "crazy," Bill implicitly knew the information was not for print.

The "price" of information probably varied with the category. For example, to obtain information on a background, off-the-record basis, Bill would have to offer trust as a commodity. That is, a source providing directly attributable information might cooperate if he could be assured of accurate reporting; but to provide off-the-record information, a source would have to be assured not only of accuracy (if the information could be used without the source's name) but of Bill's trustworthiness in keeping his mouth shut.

In addition to straight, factual information, sources might also provide explanation of something unclear to Bill, opinions or speculation, confirmation and reaction. I saw very little explanation as information. But Bill more frequently obtained confirmation, reaction and opinions and speculation from sources. Confirmation and particularly reaction information was most likely to see print; Bill very seldom quoted opinion and speculation from his sources, although he frequently solicited it on an off-the-record basis.

Probably the most important type of information sources gave Bill was tips. These consisted of two types: tips helping Bill locate other sources and tips alerting Bill to a possibly newsworthy story. The story on the judge's comments was an example of both. A tip alerted Bill to the existence of the incident, and subsequent tips ultimately helped him locate the victim and find people to fill in details of the incident.

What did Bill have to offer sources? He could and did offer them enjoyable social contact, perhaps a welcome break during the day. He might offer them the feeling of being in touch, particularly when he gave them an idea of what was happening elsewhere on his beat. Along those lines, he might offer them inside information, but as I noted earlier, Bill was reluctant to do that. He could also offer his low-key approach to gathering information and thus a much more pleasant way to impart information than if Bill were generally aggressive, antagonistic and demanding. He might offer flattery, either by way of direct compliment (which he rarely did) or merely by the fact that he had sought persons out as sources. He might offer sources the chance simply to do something altruistic—the chance to provide information that might be of public value, for example. Bill also gave sources an opportunity to ventilate about reporting they thought had been poor or biased, although they always ventilated about other reporters, never about Bill.

Bill could also offer sources his trustworthiness, competence and objectivity, and I believe he frequently, perhaps consciously, did so. For example, when he prefaced questions with "just between you and me," he was implicitly saying "you know you can trust me to be discreet," and sources frequently complied. Certainly these "commodities" were implicitly being exchanged for information when attorneys and judges made statements to Bill or in Bill's presence that they took for granted he would not publish. And, as mentioned above, Bill was extremely conscious of appearing objective and fair, and he was concomitantly concerned about how sources and others on his beat reacted to his stories.

Finally, of course, there is the publicity or potential for publicity Bill could offer his sources. This too falls into several categories. Bill might offer publicity that would be good for a source personally because it is flattering, either inherently because of something the source has done or because a story is actually slanted favorably toward the source. Related to this would be publicity that advances a source professionally either within or without an organization. For example, favorable publicity might help a lawyer add clients and build his or her practice. Or it might smooth a judge's reelection (although reelection is seldom a problem for judges). On the other hand, publicity might be either good or bad for someone else. The right kind of publicity might be good for an attorney's client; the wrong kind could be damaging. Publicity might be used or sought to achieve either revenge or justice. Finally, Bill might provide publicity that is good or bad for an agency or organization.

We must also consider why Bill's sources cooperated with him; i.e., what commodities they offered and exchanged with him.

From judges, Bill received generally friendly social contact, reasonably easy access to themselves, and information including tips, some factual information and some confirmation. In return, Bill offered judges some friendly contact, his low-key approach, some information about other action on his beat, potential and actual personal publicity, accurate reporting, an opportunity to ventilate, objectivity and trust. More specifically, when judges offered Bill tips, they certainly saw that they might see their own names in print, but they might also have seen the information as something the public needed to know. In the case of the judge's indiscreet comments, the judge in effect was able to use publicity defensively, and he did so exceptionally well. Bill also clearly was offering that judge objectivity, an opportunity to at least have his gaff presented fairly. When judges provided tips and informal conversation, they were also clearly receiving Bill's trustworthiness in return; they knew that he knew what would be on and off the record.

Prosecuting attorneys offered Bill a variety of information: tips, confirmation, reaction (both on and off the record), opinion and speculation (generally off the record and often rather vague), background information and other factual information. They also were easily accessible to Bill and provided some pleasant social contact. From Bill, they received publicity for themselves and their offices, although generally this was publicity inherent in the coverage of the court action itself. They received Bill's competent reporting, but they also were given an opportunity to ventilate—which they used—about other reporters. And, of course, they, too, received the pleasant social contact and low-key approach Bill offered.

Criminal defense attorneys provided Bill with information including tips (generally leading him to other sources who could be of more help), confirmation and reaction. They made themselves reasonably accessible to Bill and provided him with some pleasant social contact. From Bill, they received social contact, his trustworthiness and some, but very little, publicity. In fact, the only defense attorney named in any of Bill's stories was the victim of the indiscreet remark, and other defense attorneys were quoted only once (on the severity of the criminal sentences).

Court clerks provided Bill with tips on possible stories, reaction to the stories Bill wrote, some social interchange and easy access to records. In return, Bill offered the clerks some pleasant social contact, perhaps some outlet for clerks altruistically to provide the public with information, and some publicity, although not publicity for themselves (no clerk was quoted in any of Bill's stories) but publicity for cases the clerks might think interesting. Bill's trustworthiness and competence as a reporter may also have been important in making clerks willing to cooperate.

Yet, although exchange behavior occurred and the observational study confirms the sociopolitical nature of the news-making process, I saw few if any unambiguous examples of sources attempting to obtain manipulative publicity. On the contrary, many sources appeared cautious when dealing with Bill on substantive matters. Sometimes it seemed as though the good-natured banter was functional for sources not merely as a means of maintaining a pleasant relationship but for making their caution more palatable and less conspicuous. Many sources thereby passed the initiative to Bill or to other more aggressive sources, forfeiting an opportunity to exert more influence on the shape of judicial news. This may be one reason Bill gravitated particularly toward two judges who, for whatever reasons, were especially accessible and cooperative.

This is not to say that the prospect of publicity—manipulative or otherwise—was not important to some sources. The utility of publicity in one way or another must have been apparent at least to the sources whose tips led to the majority of Bill's stories. But there seemed to be very little competition among sources for Bill's attention.

This, in turn, suggests that the news-making process may be different in the judicial branch than in other branches of government. There was little evidence during my observation that any sources attempted to involve Bill in judicial decision making or policy making per se. Such motivation might be inferred from one judge's attempt to interest Bill in a court case because it involved a gruesome crime allegedly committed by a defendant on parole. But even this seems directed more at influencing corrections policy than judicial policy. Likewise, the tip that led to the story on the commissioner's memo may have had policy implications, but those implication seem political as much as judicial. Nor was there much evidence of Bill performing a significant function for sources as a communication link among them. Certainly some sources did ask Bill directly for information, but Bill was reluctant to accommodate requests for unpublished information, and my impression was that sources sought information to satisfy their curiosity more than for instrumental reasons.

There was evidence, however, that sources paid attention to Bill's stories. Besides sources' curiosity, their reasons for this attention were not obvious. In fact, it is difficult to infer what instrumental value most of the published information would have for sources. Some of Bill's published information may have been useful to sources, and the publicity given to the commissioner's memo is the clearest example. A logical inference is that the source who provided the tip for the story hoped the publicity would make it politically difficult for the commissioner to obtain the budget cut at issue. The story about the judge's comments probably stimulated the judge to be more discreet in his courtroom; but although that may have been helpful to some attorneys, it is doubtful that the judge's decision making itself would be affected.[5]

One conclusion, therefore, is that Bill himself may not have been the type of communication link among sources in the judiciary that research has suggested reporters are in other branches of government.[6] He and his stories probably did not play the same role—or at least not to the same degree—as reporters and stories in other branches of government. Sources seem to have regarded Bill first and foremost as a link to the general public.

Reporter and Source Roles

The observations suggest that although attorneys and judges both provided useful tips, their tips involved fundamentally different types of stories. The attorneys' tips seemed to have more manipulative motives.[7] Although Bill himself wrote no stories based on judges' tips, the tips judges gave him—on the criminal sexual conduct case and on the campaign law case—seemed to have less manipulative motives. The same appears to be the case with tips from clerks.[8]

This may suggest that attorneys are the most likely to fall into the "promoter" source category; at least it may indicate that they are more likely to do so than judges and clerks, who tend to be "informers" and "educators." If we assume that Bill may be categorized as a "recorder" or "expositor" type of reporter, his relationship with most of his sources ought to have been compatible. And that is what appears to be the case. This relationship can slip into a competitive one, as when an attorney source literally turned his back and walked briskly away from Bill to avoid cooperating in any way. Perhaps it is no coincidence that it was an attorney who took this stance.

In a broader sense, this suggests that the norm for press relations with judicial sources is compatibility, but that this can change quickly with circumstances.

SUMMARY

This chapter presented an observational case study of one full-time newspaper court reporter in Minnesota. The observation suggests that the reporter was strikingly dependent on personal sources for tips on news-worthy judicial activity. Although court proceedings and records are pub-lic, the reporter seemed to depend heavily on personal sources to make his large beat efficiently manageable. This made his relationship with those sources important, and would suggest that his sources might be in a relatively powerful position, at least to the degree that they need the pub-licity he can provide less than he needs their assistance. The reporter's re-lationship with almost all sources was routinely compatible.

Notes

1. See, e.g., Earl R. Babbie, *The Practice of Social Research* (Belmont, Calif.: Wadsworth, 1973), pp. 196–97. See generally, John Lofland, *Analyzing Social Settings* (Belmont, Calif.: Wadsworth, 1971). A number of other students of the news-making process have used observation as a primary method. For an example in the judicial context, see David L. Grey, "Decision-Making by a Re-porter under Deadline Pressure," *Journalism Quarterly* 43 (1966):419–28.

2. If a court story involves an issue that has been followed closely by another reporter on the staff, that reporter will frequently cover the court action, too.

3. Bill estimated that he spends no more than 25 percent of his time in the courtroom.

4. By newsworthiness, I mean such traditional attributes as importance, in-terest, proximity, the presence of prominent names, recency, magnitude and con-flict. See, e.g., Mitchell V. Charnley and Blair Charnley, *Reporting*, 4th ed. (New York: Holt, Rinehart & Winston, 1979), pp. 49–67; Michael Ryan and James W. Tankard, Jr., *Basic News Reporting* (Palo Alto: Mayfield Publishing Co., 1977), pp. 105–09; Melvin Mencher, *News Reporting and Writing* (Dubuque: Wm. C. Brown, 1977), pp. 66–72.

5. Nevertheless, even this limited result could be interpreted as a significant control exerted by the press on the judiciary.

6. See chapter 2, p. 14.

7. I am assuming that the tips on the commissioner's memo and the judge's comments came from attorneys, although Bill did not explicitly say so. Various sources said that the judge had frequently made thoughtless comments from the bench.

8. Law enforcement sources were also a part of Bill's federal building beat, although they are not judicial sources per se. It is worth noting that circumstantial evidence points to these sources cooperating for manipulative publicity reasons. The one story directly involving those sources came from a tip, and previous pub-licity was posted on an office wall.

5

Reporter-Source Interaction in Minnesota Trial Courts

Chapters 1 and 2 set out the descriptive and more theoretical aims of this research and spun the rationale for it. This chapter and chapter 6 present the results of a questionnaire survey designed specifically to gather data about judicial sources and newspaper reporters and their interaction in Minnesota trial courts. This chapter focuses on the mechanics of the interaction—the reporters' and sources' demographic characteristics, the frequency of their interaction, the type of help sources provide, how cooperative they are, how frequently they seek out reporters and what complaints sources and reporters have about each other. Chapter 6 considers reasons why sources cooperate and what roles they and reporters consider appropriate for the press as it covers the trial courts.

Attorneys, judges, court clerks and daily newspaper reporters were surveyed. The three types of sources were selected because they are the most likely to have significant contact with reporters. Law enforcement sources were excluded because they are not considered part of the judicial branch. The goal was to gather data that provide a picture of routine news making in the trial courts and from which a better understanding of that process and its implications may be attained.

METHOD

The questionnaire was prepared, pretested, revised and then administered to municipal, county and district judges,[1] clerks of court, county attorneys, public defenders and private attorneys in Minnesota in late 1979 and early 1980. Newspaper reporters were surveyed in early 1980. Questionnaires were tailored to the type of respondent but contained several identical questions.

Response rate, particularly from judges and attorneys, was perceived as a potentially serious problem. Other researchers have had difficulty obtaining response from such groups.[2] This problem was solved thanks to cooperation from the Minnesota Supreme Court Office of Continuing Education for State Court Personnel, the County Attorneys Council and the Minnesota Bar Association's Continuing Legal Education. The Supreme Court office not only provided a cover letter (in addition to my own) from its director urging cooperation from clerks and judges but also duplicated and mailed questionnaires to all state judges and clerks of court, collected returned questionnaires and handled follow-up. Consequently, completed questionnaires were received from 137 of 207 judges (66 percent). More specifically, 16 of 28 municipal judges (57 percent), 70 of 107 county judges (65 percent) and 51 of 72 district judges (71 percent) responded. Response from clerks of court was 66 of 87 (76 percent).

County attorneys were surveyed to obtain responses from attorneys who do criminal prosecution work. The executive director of the County Attorneys Council provided a cover letter urging cooperation and also handled follow-up. Questionnaires were mailed to 99 county attorneys and assistant county attorneys in Minnesota's 87 counties.[3] Responses were obtained from county attorneys in 59 counties (68 percent) and from 66 of those surveyed (67 percent).

Public defenders were surveyed to obtain the views of criminal defense attorneys. I contacted the chief public defender in each judicial district by phone to obtain names and addresses of his assistants. Questionnaires were mailed to 87 public defenders and 63 (71 percent) responded.[4]

Reaching private practice attorneys presented the most difficult problem. A mail questionnaire seemed particularly vulnerable to poor response rate. Further, according to data from the Minnesota Supreme Court, approximately 8850 attorneys practice in the state. The best alternative seemed to be administering questionnaires in person to a relatively captive audience. Continuing Legal Education agreed to administer questionnaires to attorneys at two workshops, thus allowing me to obtain response from attorneys not primarily involved in criminal practice. Data were obtained from 64 private practice attorneys. One set of questionnaires was administered at a session on family law; a second set at a workshop on debtor-creditor law. About 72 percent of the attorneys reported practicing in counties of 100,000 or more, which means they practice in the Twin Cities metropolitan area or in St. Louis County (which includes Duluth). This appears to be good representation in terms of population since the Minnesota Bar Association estimates that at least 67 percent of the state's attorneys practice in the Hennepin-Ramsey area which includes Minneapolis and St. Paul.[5] Obviously, I cannot claim that this sample is statistically representative of all private practice attorneys in Minnesota, only that it is a purposive sample with some randomness.[6]

Daily newspaper court reporters were surveyed after I obtained their names from editors. Questionnaires were mailed to all 31 reporters who cover courts. After follow-up, 24 had responded (77 percent). The 31 reporters from whom I had hoped to receive data represented 29 newspapers. The 24 respondents represented 23 newspapers (79 percent of the newspapers). The results were coded and computer-processed.[7]

DEMOGRAPHICS

The respondents came from counties varying considerably in population.[8] The clerks and county attorneys are skewed toward smaller counties— those with populations less than 30,000—because their positions are tied to county seats. Public defenders and private attorneys are skewed more toward larger counties—those of 100,000 or more—and that is understandable because those are areas with the heaviest caseloads. In fact, about 50 percent of the state's population lives in the Minneapolis–St. Paul area alone. Judges are more difficult to categorize because many serve more than one county. Reporter respondents tended to come from counties of less than 30,000 or more than 50,000. Roughly two-thirds worked for newspapers circulating less than 20,000 papers; another fifth worked for papers of 100,000 circulation or more.

Table 5.1 shows that sources and reporters differed dramatically in terms of job experience. Compared to sources, reporters were greenhorns.[9] The difference is even greater if we consider that nearly half the court clerks held similar positions before assuming their present jobs and that more than 90 percent of the judges had practiced law for six or more years before assuming the bench.[10] As might be expected, the reporters were also young—three-fourths of them less than 30 and only one more than 50. Clearly, many of the reporters were on their first full-time

TABLE 5.1 Percentage of Respondents with Various Years of Work Experience

	Years of Experience*						
Respondent Type	Less than 1	1–5	6–10	11–15	More than 15	Total	Number of Cases
Clerks	9%	29%	30%	15%	17%	100%	66
Judges	5	26	25	21	23	100	137
County attorneys	0	26	38	18	18	100	66
Public defenders	6	38	29	14	13	100	63
Private attorneys	14	48	13	11	14	100	64
Reporters	57	35	0	4	4	100	23

* Clerks' responses refer to years in present position, judges' to years on bench, attorneys' to years practicing law and reporters' to years covering courts.

job in the field. But they were well educated. All had graduated from high school and 88 percent had college degrees, including three who had done graduate work. Seventy percent (14) of those with college degrees had majored in journalism or mass communication; another 20 percent (4) listed their majors as English or literature.[11] Two had done graduate work in English, one in psychology. But 75 percent said they had no training of any kind in law. The remainder indicated having various undergraduate classes related to law, including mass communication law.

Compared with other journalists in communities of similar sizes, the Minnesota court reporters are better-educated and more likely to have studied journalism.[12] But compared with reporters covering the U.S. Supreme Court and/or a Washington law beat, the Minnesotans are significantly younger and less experienced, and their education is less specialized.[13] For example, Hess found that nearly two-thirds of the law reporters in his Washington study had graduate degrees; and Dennis found that a half-dozen of the reporters covering the U.S. Supreme Court had law degrees.[14]

Given the gap between the trial court reporters' and sources' experience, educations and ages,[15] one might expect some problems. Inexperienced reporters, unsophisticated in the technicalities of law, might be particularly vulnerable not only to error but to manipulation by sources. If the specialists covering the U.S. Supreme Court have been criticized for incompetence, how should the relative novice at the trial court level be expected to perform? Sources, with their highly specialized, technical orientation might also overreact to the reporters' attempts to write for a lay audience. News stories are not court decisions or briefs, but judicial sources may be inclined to read and analyze them as though they were. Finally, legal training and journalistic training may themselves set reporters and sources on a collision course to the degree that the former is client-oriented, while the latter is somewhat more society-oriented. We can see this distinction emerge in the fair trial–free press debate when bench and bar frame the issue in terms of defendants' rights, while journalists argue on behalf of the public. These differing orientations may affect reporter-source relationships and produce tension and constriction of information flow.

CONTACT WITH REPORTERS

Nearly all the clerks (97 percent) and judges (95 percent) and all the county attorneys said they had been contacted by a local newspaper reporter. But the number drops to 79 percent of the public defenders and only 59 percent of the private attorneys. Table 5.2 focuses on how often sources said they had been contacted by a local newspaper reporter during the past six months.

TABLE 5.2 Percentage of Sources Indicating Frequency of Contact with Reporters During Past Six Months

Source Type	None	At Least Once	Weekly	Daily	Total*	Number of Cases
		Frequency of Contact				
Clerks[†] (personally)	3%	50%	40%	7%	100%	60
Clerks' office[‡]	0	32	56	13	101	63
Judges	10	76	13	1	100	129
All attorneys	14	68	18	0	100	150
County attorneys	2	58	41	0	101	64
Public defenders	19	81	0	0	100	48
Private attorneys	29	68	3	0	100	38

* Some totals exceed 100% due to rounding.
† Refers only to personal contact with clerk of court.
‡ Refers to contact with anyone in clerks' office.

The reporters' preference for clerks and county attorneys is obvious if not overwhelming. Perhaps this is because these are the most accessible and convenient sources—clerks because their offices are the repository for court records and have the best total view of what is occurring in court, county attorneys because of their crucial role in the criminal process and because as elected officials they have an incentive not only to convict defendants but to seek personal publicity. Because newspapers pay the most attention to criminal cases, because prosecutors have access to much information that reporters need and need quickly and because prosecutors have an incentive to cooperate, they are sources of considerable strategic value to reporters.

Reporters' penchant for criminal cases would seem to explain why private attorneys receive so little attention, especially when private attorneys have relatively little incentive to cooperate anyway. What is less clear is why judges and public defenders report so little contact with reporters. Judges simply may not have much information that reporters need, nor may they have much incentive to seek contact with journalists for personal, manipulative reasons. Some reporters may also be uncomfortable about approaching judges because they are intimidated by the judges' office. But what about public defenders? Since the fundamental canons of American journalism include objectivity, fairness and balance, why don't reporters seek out criminal defense attorneys as much as prosecutors? One possibility is that reporters have found such sources uncooperative, or so clearly expect them to be uncooperative, that they don't bother trying. Another is that these attorneys just don't seek publicity. After all, one seldom if ever hears complaints from bench and bar that press coverage is prejudicially favorable to a defendant. Yet another possibility is that public defenders physically may be hard to contact since they, unlike other sources, do not all maintain daily offices in the town where the newspaper is published. Such accessibility difficulties are seriously inefficient for reporters. Of course, one other explanation might be that journalists simply aren't cognizant of the one-sidedness that may result from such heavy reliance on prosecutors.

As table 5.3 indicates, reporters generally confirm what sources say about their contact. Note, too, how much contact court reporters have with law enforcement officials. This, coupled with reporters' reliance on prosecutors, would seem to create conditions conducive to coverage favorable to the prosecution and perhaps alienate defense attorneys as sources. The reporters' responses also indicate how heavily they use court documents; nor should this be surprising since documents are accessible, convenient and efficient sources.

TABLE 5.3 Percentage of Reporters Indicating Frequency of Contact with Source Types During Past Six Months

Source Type*	Frequency of Contact					Number of Cases
	Never	At Least Once	Weekly	Daily	Total†	
Clerks	0%	8%	54%	38%	100%	24
Judges	4	58	29	8	99	24
Prosecutors	0	52	44	4	100	23
Criminal defense attorneys	4	79	13	4	100	24
Other attorneys	17	63	21	0	101	24
Criminal defendants	67	29	4	0	100	24
Noncriminal litigants	35	52	13	0	100	23
Official court reporter	38	42	17	4	101	24
Law enforcement officials	4	46	29	21	100	24
Bailiffs	70	17	13	0	100	23
Petit jurors	75	25	0	0	100	24
Grand jurors	96	4	0	0	100	23
Witnesses	50	46	4	0	100	24
Documents	0	0	54	46	100	24
Legal reference books	13	65	17	4	99	23
Legal experts‡	71	29	0	0	100	24
Other news reporters	54	38	8	0	100	24

* Reporters were not asked to distinguish state from federal court sources.

† Some totals do not equal 100% due to rounding.

‡ The reporters were given law professors as one example of this type of source in order to clarify the question.

If reporters need sources that are efficient because they provide useful information quickly and cooperatively with a minimum expenditure of reporter time and effort, we shouldn't be surprised if reporters spend little time in courtrooms. Observation is, above all, time-consuming; the payoff must be large to justify the time required. In fact, sources and reporters confirm that only a minority of judicial news comes from courtroom observation.

When asked during what percentage of their own appearances in court during the past six months the clerks and attorneys had noticed the presence of local newspaper reporters, more than 80 percent said less than a fourth of the time.[16] Nearly two-thirds of the private attorneys said never. Even a fourth of the judges reported not having seen a local reporter in court. The reporters indicated that an average of 29 percent of all the court information they gather comes from observing court proceedings.[17] This lack of firsthand observation may also constrict the growth of reporters' personal sources. One of the better opportunities for reporters to meet public defenders and private attorneys may be lost, and reporters are thus all the more likely to rely on sources available at accessible local offices—namely county attorneys, clerks and law enforcement officials.

HELP SOUGHT AND HELP PROVIDED

What do reporters want from judicial sources, and what will these sources give them? The questionnaire asked sources whether or not reporters had sought the following specified types of information or assistance during the past six months, and then whether they either had provided or would provide such help. Reporters were asked whether, during the past six months, they had asked each type of source for the same types of information, and whether they had in fact obtained such information from those sources. Tables 5.4, 5.5, 5.6 and 5.7 show the results.

Factual information about a case.   Obviously, obtaining facts is a prime goal of reporters, and that is what the data show. Although most sources are asked and would provide such help, the county attorneys are the favorite and most willing choice. In this regard, they differed strikingly from the other attorneys, who were more reluctant to cooperate. This may reflect the county attorneys' accessibility and crucial position in the criminal process and also explain in part why reporters less frequently contact public defenders and other attorneys. But it may also suggest that county attorneys have the most to gain by cooperating; the facts on which criminal cases are prosecuted seldom make defendants look good.

Explanation of legal technicalities, legal language or the judicial process itself.   County attorneys appear to be the favored source for such in-

TABLE 5.4   Percentage of Sources Who Have Been Asked by Reporters for Various Types of Assistance During Past Six Months*

Type of Assistance	Source Type					
	Clerks	Judges	All Attys.	County Attys.	Public Defenders	Private Attys.
Factual information about a case	89% (62)	75% (117)	93% (131)	100% (65)	93% (41)	76% (25)
Explanation of legal technicalities, legal language or the judicial process itself	57 (60)	82 (116)	80 (131)	85 (65)	73 (41)	80 (25)
Source's opinion about some aspect of a case or speculation about its outcome	29 (58)	25 (117)	56 (131)	60 (65)	54 (41)	48 (25)
Suggestions steering reporter to stories	25 (59)	33 (116)	43 (128)	53 (64)	25 (40)	46 (24)
Help deciding whether a case will be worth coverage	24 (59)	16 (116)	16 (129)	19 (65)	15 (40)	13 (24)
Explanation of something source has done in handling a particular case	31 (59)	73 (117)	71 (130)	77 (65)	66 (41)	63 (24)
Help confirming accuracy of something reporter has written or is writing	61 (59)	62 (117)	72 (130)	82 (65)	55 (40)	76 (25)
An interview for a judicial story, but not related to coverage of a particular case	34 (59)	59 (117)	37 (127)	52 (65)	18 (40)	27 (22)
Access to and/or copying of court records	77 (61)	47 (116)	31 (129)	45 (65)	18 (40)	17 (24)
Nothing in particular; just a chat	56 (52)	49 (99)	50 (115)	56 (57)	46 (37)	43 (21)

* Numbers in parentheses indicate number of cases on which percentage is based.

TABLE 5.5 Percentage of Sources Who Have Provided or Would Provide Various Types of Assistance to Reporters*

Type of Assistance	Source Type					
	Clerks	Judges	All Attys.	County Attys.	Public Defenders	Private Attys.
Factual information about a case	88% (58)	76% (127)	75% (185)	92% (62)	71% (62)	62% (61)
Explanation of legal technicalities, legal language or the judicial process itself	55 (58)	95 (131)	93 (182)	95 (63)	89 (61)	95 (58)
Source's opinion about some aspect of a case or speculation about its outcome	7 (60)	9 (128)	25 (185)	29 (62)	24 (62)	21 (61)
Suggestions steering reporter to stories	39 (59)	46 (129)	49 (182)	62 (63)	41 (61)	43 (58)
Help deciding whether a case will be worth coverage	33 (60)	42 (126)	47 (181)	48 (61)	39 (61)	54 (59)
Explanation of something source has done in handling a particular case	65 (60)	86 (126)	75 (181)	90 (62)	69 (61)	64 (58)
Help confirming accuracy of something reporter has written or is writing	88 (59)	89 (127)	84 (176)	93 (61)	75 (60)	84 (55)
An interview for a judicial story, but not related to coverage of a particular case	62 (58)	94 (129)	86 (183)	87 (63)	80 (61)	92 (59)
Access to and/or copying of court records	98 (58)	89 (130)	55 (177)	68 (62)	55 (58)	40 (57)
Nothing in particular; just a chat	89 (55)	93 (121)	88 (165)	91 (57)	82 (54)	91 (54)

* Numbers in parentheses indicate number of cases on which percentage is based.

TABLE 5.6 Percentage of Reporters Who Asked Sources for Various Types of Assistance During Past Six Months

Type of Assistance	Clerks	Judges	Prosecutors	Criminal Defense Attys.	Other Attys.	Number of Cases
Factual information about a case	92%*	79%	96%	83%	54%	24
Explanation of legal technicalities, legal language or the judicial process itself	50	79	83	54	50	24
Source's opinion about some aspect of a case or speculation about its outcome	39	39	57	48	30	23
Suggestions steering reporter to stories	58	58	58	38	46	24
Help deciding whether a case will be worth coverage	48	52	48	17	22	23
Explanation of something source has done in handling a particular case	33	71	79	67	42	24
Help confirming accuracy of something reporter has written or is writing	54	46	83	50	38	24
An interview for a judicial story, but not related to coverage of a particular case	39	61	52	44	52	23
Access to and/or copying of court records	96	46	54	17	21	24
Nothing in particular; just a chat	75	79	75	58	63	24

* Table should be read as follows: 92% of reporters have asked clerks for factual information about a case.

NOTE: Reporters were not asked to distinguish federal from state sources.

TABLE 5.7 Percentage of Reporters Who Received Various Types of Assistance from Sources During Past Six Months

Type of Assistance	Clerks	Judges	Prosecutors	Criminal Defense Attys.	Other Attys.	Number of Cases
Factual information about a case	88%*	79%	100%	83%	46%	24
Explanation of legal technicalities, legal language or the judicial process itself	54	83	88	58	46	24
Source's opinion about some aspect of a case or speculation about its outcome	48	35	44	39	30	23
Suggestions steering reporter to stories	67	63	54	33	38	24
Help deciding whether a case will be worth coverage	48	48	44	22	26	23
Explanation of something source has done in handling a particular case	33	67	75	58	42	24
Help confirming accuracy of something reporter has written or is writing	55	50	82	50	41	22
An interview for a judicial story, but not related to coverage of a particular case	38	58	54	33	46	24
Access to and/or copying of court records	83	46	54	25	21	24
Nothing in particular; just a chat	79	79	71	58	63	24

* Table should be read as follows: 88% of reporters have received factual information about a case from clerks.

NOTE: Reporters were not asked to distinguish federal from state sources.

formation also, although the differences among sources is very small. The exception is the clerks, who are notably less willing to provide such help, but that is understandable since they would seem to have the least legal expertise. The results indicate that judges and attorneys are very willing to provide such help. In fact, more of them are willing to provide such help than have been asked. This implies that these sources are cognizant of the value of having the public understand the judicial system. It may also imply sources' concern that reporters may not clearly understand the system and its procedure.

Source's opinion about some aspect of a case or speculation about how it will turn out. If we were discussing sources in the legislative or executive branches and decisions made there, we would hardly expect sources to be reluctant to talk. But in the judicial branch, as I suggested in chapter 2, the situation is different and such cooperation is less likely. Not surprisingly, the data confirm that the vast majority of sources are reluctant to provide such information. And the majority of reporters appear reluctant even to ask for it. It is true that more county attorneys than any other source say they will provide such information, but the percentage is small. The reporters' responses seem to indicate that sources are more willing to provide such comment than they admit. However, since the number of reporters is small, it may be that in absolute numbers only a handful of sources provide such information.

Suggestions steering the reporter to possible stories. More sources are willing to provide such assistance than are asked, and once again the county attorneys are favored and willing sources. This may be because county attorneys have a good vantage point from which to spot newsworthy matters; but it may also be because most criminal case publicity—right from the time of arrest and charging—seems inherently to favor the prosecution. Nevertheless, most sources indicated reluctance to suggest stories, and this supports the argument that judicial sources are generally less aggressive than other government sources. The reporters' responses indicate that sources may suggest more stories than they admit, but again a small number of aggressive sources could have skewed the results.

Help in deciding whether a particular case will be worth newspaper coverage. The response here provides more evidence for the position that most judicial sources are not particularly aggressive in trying to shape the nature of judicial coverage. That few sources say they have been asked for such assistance may simply reflect reporters' reluctance to defer to others' news judgment; or coupled with the fact that more than half the reporters said they had received such help from clerks, judges and prosecutors, it may suggest that those sources who are aggressive can be effective. The plausibility of the latter is enhanced if we compare the percentage of reporters who say they've sought such help with the percentage of sources who say they've been asked. The reporters' responses also indicate again a preference for sources other than criminal defense attorneys and civil practice attorneys.

Explanation of something [a source] has done in handling a particular case. Taken together, the reporter and source responses indicate that such information can flow quite smoothly. That more county attorneys and judges are willing to provide such assistance may be related to their positions as elected officials. They may feel an obligation, if not a practical need, to explain to voters what they are doing; their reasons may or may not be manipulative. Nevertheless, more of every source type than are asked would be willing to provide such help, and there is no reason to have expected otherwise.[18]

Help in confirming the accuracy of something the reporter is writing or has written. Clearly, sources are willing to provide such help—apparently more willing to provide it than reporters are to seek it. This isn't surprising, especially since the press has been criticized for inaccurate judicial reporting. Despite all sources' willingness, reporters gravitate toward the county attorneys.

An interview with [a source] for a newspaper story on a topic involving the courts or a legal issue, but not related to the reporter's coverage of a particular case. Since press coverage of the courts has been criticized for being superficial, one would expect sources to be happy to provide this type of help; that is exactly what the results show. The sources' response suggests that county attorneys are yet again the favorite source for reporters, an indication perhaps that these officials are in a strong position to shape not only coverage of cases but also of other legal issues.

Access to and/or copying of a court document or record. The results confirm that clerks are the obvious source for such assistance. Clerks and judges are both willing to provide access, but attorneys are more reluctant. Perhaps this is because attorneys did not distinguish public from nonpublic records[19] or because they believed providing such access was not their responsibility. Of the attorneys, the county attorneys appear more willing to provide access; again it may be because the county attorney is an elected official and because information in documents is likely to help more than hinder the prosecution.

Nothing in particular—just a friendly chat. This item was included primarily as an indicator of how generally accessible sources are. The response suggests that they are quite accessible. It also suggests that reporters are not taking full advantage of the potential. And since such contact may lead to sound and useful reporter-source relationships, the information that could flow from such relationships is forfeited.[20]

Reporters were also asked to rate sources on a scale of uncooperative, cooperative or very cooperative. Table 5.8 shows the results.

TABLE 5.8 Percentage of Reporters Rating Sources as Uncooperative, Cooperative or Very Cooperative*

Source Type†	Reporters' Rating				Number of Cases
	Uncooperative	Cooperative	Very Cooperative	Total	
Clerks	0%	42%	58%	100%	24
Judges	0	41	59	100	22
Prosecutors	17	35	48	100	23
Criminal defense attorneys	14	68	18	100	22
Other attorneys	5	70	25	100	20

* The exact question was, "Generally speaking, how would you rate the overall cooperativeness of each of the following sources?"
† Reporters were not asked to distinguish federal from state court sources.

Obviously, the reporters find sources to be generally cooperative, a finding that suggests that the sometimes acrimonious disputes between bench, bar and press should not be taken for the norm. Routine judicial source-reporter relationships may not be nearly as bad as some egregious cases imply. The rocky relationships reporters had were exclusively with attorneys—and those are the sources I suggested in chapter 2 would be most likely to manipulate publicity, although I suggested this might not be common. Attempts to manipulate publicity—or the lack of it—can place sources in Nimmo's "promoter" category. When such sources encounter reporters, the result can be strained relations. Such may be reflected here.

It is one thing for a source to cooperate with a reporter when asked; but how often do judicial sources actually seek out reporters to offer unsolicited information? Table 5.9 indicates that most sources are not very aggressive in pursuit of coverage.

TABLE 5.9 Percentage of Sources Who Have Sought Out Local Newspaper Reporter with Unsolicited Information or Explanation

Source Type	Have Sought	Have Not Sought	Total*	Number of Cases
Clerks	22%	78%	100%	64
Judges	17	83	100	134
All attorneys	22	79	101	191
County attorneys	39	61	100	66
Public defenders	16	84	100	63
Private attorneys	8	92	100	62

* Totals do not all equal 100% due to rounding.

This is consistent with the position that judicial sources do not need publicity the same way as sources in other branches of government.[21] The county attorneys appear to be the most aggressive sources, providing yet another indication of their potential influence on judicial news and of why reporters rely heavily on them. Still, less than half the county attorneys said they had sought out reporters.

The reporters' responses somewhat belie the sources', however, as table 5.10 shows.

TABLE 5.10   Percentage of Reporters Indicating How Frequently Sources Offered Unsolicited Information, Tips or Story Ideas During Past Six Months

Source Type*	Never	Rarely	Occasionally	Frequently	Total†	Number of Cases
Clerks	13%	33%	33%	21%	100%	24
Judges	27	32	36	5	100	22
Prosecutors	21	38	25	17	101	24
Criminal defense attorneys	29	52	19	0	100	21
Other attorneys	33	33	33	0	99	21

* Reporters were not asked to distinguish state from federal sources.
† Totals do not all equal 100% due to rounding.

Reporters indicate that sources are more aggressive than sources admit. Further, 57 percent of the reporters said that during the previous six months sources' unsolicited tips led to stories for them. And nearly half the reporters said that leaks—the unauthorized release of otherwise non-public information—had been occasional or frequent; only 17 percent of the reporters said they had never received a judicial leak.

Although sources may in fact have underreported their activity, another explanation is that the reporters' response was inflated by the aggressiveness of a very few sources. If so, that only reemphasizes how much impact aggressive sources can have in a system in which most sources are passive. The reporters do confirm the relative inactivity of criminal defense attorneys and other attorneys, perhaps some indication of who should bear the primary blame for "trying cases in the newspapers."

ERRORS AND COMPLAINTS

Sources were asked in what percentage of news stories about cases they have handled—or, in the case of clerks, cases of which they have firsthand knowledge—they notice factual inaccuracies. Between one-fourth and one-third of all judges and attorneys said they have seen factual errors in half or more of all such stories. Another fifth of judges and attorneys said they have noticed errors in 25 to 49 percent of such stories. The mode for all groups, including clerks, was noticing errors in 1 to 24 percent of the stories. Relatively few sources reported never noticing an error. Judges and attorneys noticed errors in a greater percentage of stories than clerks.

One might assume, then, that sources' biggest complaint about reporters might be inaccuracy, and in fact that is precisely what most sources said when asked what, if anything, was their biggest complaint about newspaper coverage, based on their personal experience. Table 5.11 shows the array of responses. Lack of knowledge about the judicial process, bias and sensationalism were also commonly mentioned by all sources, and frequently their complaints combined two or more of these gripes.

Wrote one judge:

> The paper takes a position and will do its best not to reverse its stand. A newspaper may be wrong, but they are never in doubt. Papers will do anything to sell papers and seem to be going overboard to embarrass judges and degrade our judicial system at a time in history when this branch of government needs public support and constructive criticism, not a public reprimand based on a reporter's personal sense of justice.

Added another:

> In addition to frequent inaccuracies, news stories by their nature are prone to be incomplete. They frequently, although probably unintentionally, create misimpressions by what they leave out as well as by what they include; they tend to emphasize what is superficial in an effort to glamorize what is innately prosaic. The efforts to educate reporters never filter through to editors and headline writers. Few cases readily lend themselves to the paraphrasing and summarizing that newspapers require.

One clerk of court covered nearly every possibility. The clerk's biggest complaint?

> A gross disregard for and indifference toward accuracy in reporting the facts. The astonishing inability of reporters to distinguish between fact and opinion. Misquoting their source so completely that it comes out the exact opposite of what was actually said. Prejudging, or deciding in advance what their story will be and then trying to make the facts fit their story. Being rude, arrogant and overbearing toward court personnel and litigants. Seeking only the sensational or the sordid or the evil, and failing to find it, playing fast and loose with the truth to make it so anyway. Slanting every story to make the justice system look bad, and then demanding the assistance of court personnel in supplying information with which to write the story. Using "freedom of the press" to justify running roughshod over an individual's right to privacy. Callousness toward the people involved in their stories. etc. etc.

TABLE 5.11 Percentage of Sources Citing "Biggest" Complaint about Newspaper Court Reporting*

Type of Complaint	Clerks	Judges	All Attys.	County Attys.	Public Defenders	Private Attys.
Reporters lack knowledge about judicial system	12%	16%	9%	8%	6%	15%
Inaccurate reporting	23	37	30	25	38	28
Biased reporting	2	17	16	4	18	28
Sensationalism	8	15	16	20	14	15
Reporter laziness	13	0	4	10	2	0
Interference with fair trial	0	1	7	14	6	0
Too little coverage	0	0	9	4	12	13
Reporters are obnoxious	8	0	0	0	0	0
Reporters/newspapers fail to correct errors	0	1	0	0	0	0
Specifically said "no complaint"	35	14	8	16	4	3
	101%†	101%	99%	101%	100%	102%
	(n = 52)	(n = 95)	(n = 141)	(n = 51)	(n = 50)	(n = 40)

* The exact question was, "What is your biggest complaint, if any, about newspaper court reporting in light of your personal experience with reporters and newspapers?"
† All totals do not equal 100% due to rounding.

A county attorney complained that reporters are interested in sensationalism, not accuracy, and that "they arrive with the idea that they are all another 'Watergate reporter' and are going to have an expose. I stay as far away as I can." Another county attorney said he was bothered by reporters' "subjective claim that the people have a 'right to know.'" "Interestingly enough," he continued, "I have never had a nonreporter come to me for information stating [that] he/she had the right to know." And from a private attorney came the complaint that "a reporter cannot explain in 30 seconds or one page what a lawyer has spent months preparing. The result is oversimplification to the point [that] the report is more inaccurate than accurate."

A number of those who complained about bias or one-sided coverage complained specifically about reporters' reliance on self-interested sources, particularly their reliance on county attorneys. One judge pointedly complained that "our local paper allows itself to be used by the county attorney." Not surprisingly, public defenders were especially vociferous in this regard. Wrote one:

> In criminal matters, too often there is a politically based pipeline moving between the prosecutor's office and the newspaper. Hence, the public gets a slanted and politically popular view of "getting" the "criminal" without knowing why a result should have been different, or even that the result may have been different.

Complained another: "I am aware of a number of prosecutors who solicit stories, who plant stories, and [of] reporters who follow them as if to lean on their every word. I find this reprehensible."[22] Although he may not have been referring to other county attorneys, one county attorney himself noted that "I wish that the press . . . would make a good faith effort to stay away from unduly attaching themselves to particular lawyers or causes."

Perhaps, then, it should not be surprising that only two county attorneys specifically listed biased stories as their major complaint, that of all the attorneys, the fewest county attorneys complained about there being too little court coverage, and that more county attorneys than other attorneys specifically stated that they had no complaints. On the other hand, county attorneys were the largest group complaining about press coverage causing fair trial problems. Only one judge clearly complained about this problem. Considering how much attention is focused on fair trial–free press conflicts, it is amazing how little concern sources expressed about it. This may indicate just how unrepresentative such conflicts are.

Comparison is profitable at this point with the reporters' listing of their most frustrating problems in covering trial courts. Actually, there was relatively little variation in the reporters' complaints, and they may be summarized as follows:

Complaint	Number of Mentions	Percentage
Officials uncooperative	1	5.6
Lack of time to do adequate job	9	50.0
Legalese	2	11.1
False mystique surrounding judicial system	2	11.1
Sources attempt to bias outcomes	1	5.6
Lack of knowledge by reporter	1	5.6
Miscellaneous	2	11.1

Obviously lack of time was the biggest problem. As one reporter wrote, "[There are] too many possible good articles. It's a constant frustration to pass up some stories because of lack of time." Some sources apparently recognize and even sympathize with this problem. "Rural newspapers hire low paid reporters and overwork them," wrote one judge. "Thus they aren't trained or knowledgeable about how to gather information. Reports thus come from one party, one attorney, or rumors with no perspective." Wrote another: "The severe understaffing by the [town's] newspapers of the reporters assigned to the court system makes it impossible for even conscientious, objective reporters to devote the time to a particular case that would result in an accurate news story." A county attorney noted that "just when they [reporters] begin to understand what they are writing about, a new reporter arrives on the beat and continues the fairly inaccurate reporting on facts and the law." Added another: "The newspapers here pay so little that a reporter is never here long enough to understand the system."

But while many sources complained about inaccuracy, incompleteness, bias, sensationalism, and lack of knowledge by reporters, few reporters mentioned these concerns. On the other hand, several reporters complained about the blameworthiness of judicial sources. "Egos" is how one reporter described his biggest frustration: "A courthouse is filled with attorneys and professional people eager to be printed. However, they are not willing to have legal jargon printed in layman's terms." Another biggest frustration was "private practice lawyers who refuse to comment on cases and lie or mislead [a] reporter by saying something is not worthy of coverage. The result is usually the reverse of inattention." Wrote a third reporter:

> [My] biggest problem has to do with civil cases; once resolved in court, attorneys from either side seem reluctant to give out much information about the case and the award (if any); this also goes for obtaining information for out-of-court settlements.

Only one reporter mentioned feeling a need to know more about the judicial process. Only one mentioned feeling torn between the need to develop good stories and the possibility of interfering with a fair trial.

In light of sources' complaints and reporters' frustrations, it is relevant to consider more of the data reporters provided about their work.

Seven-eighths of the reporters have duties in addition to court coverage, and of those reporters, 57 percent say they spend 75 percent or more of their time on noncourt duties. Another fifth spend between 50 and 74 percent of their time on noncourt assignments. Noncourt duties include local government reporting, general assignment, police reporting, education, military reporting and sports.

The reporters cover municipal, county and state district courts regularly. But there is a notable difference in the types of cases to which reporters attend. About two-thirds of the reporters spend half or more of their court-reporting time on criminal cases, but only an eighth spend that much time on civil cases. In addition, half the reporters say they spend half or more of their court-reporting time on spot news stories about cases; only two (8 percent) spend that much time on feature stories about the judiciary.

Such data would seem to explain why sources often find coverage lacking or incomplete; it also illustrates why so many reporters feel so constrained by time.

It is fortunate for reporters so limited by time that judicial action generates voluminous public documents which are efficiently centralized and easily accessible. It is not surprising that when asked to estimate how much court information they gather by various techniques, the reporters say the largest amount, 49 percent, comes from documents.[23] Just over 28 percent of their information comes from observation of court proceedings,[24] and another 20 percent from interviewing.[25] No other significant sources of information emerged.[26] Thus it would appear that reporters are relatively nondependent on personal sources in the judiciary, but this measure is quantitative, not qualitative—and quality may be the more crucial element.

One other factor with a bearing on complaints by sources and frustrations by reporters may be the influence of such factors as competition from other reporters, editors' orders, and general newspaper policy. Reporters were asked to indicate whether each of these factors affected their choice of what to cover "not at all," "some," or "a great deal." Their response clearly shows that general newspaper policy is the most important. Roughly 63 percent of the reporters said general policy influenced them "a great deal"; only 14 percent said the same for editors' orders; and only 9 percent said the same for competition. Another 17 percent said policy had "some" effect; 50 percent said the same for editors' orders; and just over 30 percent said the same for competition. Obviously, these factors, too, bear on the time reporters have to cover the courts; and sources should be aware of these potential impingements on reporter autonomy.

Notes

1. Municipal courts have jurisdiction in civil cases up to $6000, misdemeanors, city ordinance violations and the like. These courts exist only in the Minneapolis–St. Paul metropolitan counties of Hennepin and Ramsey. County courts hear civil cases up to $5000, misdemeanors, ordinance violations, traffic cases, juvenile actions, mental commitments, probate and divorce actions. District courts handle larger civil cases, gross misdemeanors and felonies, and have some overlapping jurisdiction with county courts.

2. Berkson, for example, obtained less than 30 percent response from judges, 33 percent from private attorneys. Larry C. Berkson, *The Supreme Court and Its Publics* (Lexington, Mass.: Lexington Books, 1978), p. 114.

3. Generally, one questionnaire was sent to each county; but additional questionnaires were sent to county attorney offices in six heavily populated counties, the number being suggested by the executive director of the County Attorneys Council.

4. The population of public defenders is somewhat larger than 87. The difference exists because not each of the 40 Hennepin and 27 Ramsey county public defenders was surveyed. This decision was made in consultation with officials in those offices.

5. Telephone interview with Tim Groshens, Minnesota Bar Association, Minneapolis, Minnesota, 31 July 1980.

6. The workshops were selected in consultation with the director of Continuing Legal Education who suggested that these workshops would probably attract a good cross section of state private practice attorneys. It should be noted, too, that at least some county attorneys have private practices on the side, and that some public defenders do noncriminal defense work. Thus their opinions may also somewhat reflect those of private practice attorneys.

7. Cross tabulations were run to control for a number of variables, but no significant differences emerged except among the three basic types of attorneys. The following variables were checked to see whether differences would emerge: whether judges were elected or appointed; judges' years on the bench; frequency of judges' contact with newspaper reporters; judges' type of prior law practice; judges' amount of disagreement with reporters; type of judge; community (county) size in which judge works; population of counties in which clerks work; who sets media policy in clerks' offices; clerks' amount of disagreement with reporters'; clerks' years on job; attorney type; length of attorneys' practice; amount of attorneys' contact with reporters; amount of attorneys' disagreement with reporters; size of community (county) in which attorneys practice. Tests for statistical significance are not presented in chapters 5 and 6 because the respondent groups constituted distinct populations, and in some cases the universes were surveyed in order to obtained useful numbers of responses.

8. See appendix B, table B.1.

9. This is true even if we include reporters' noncourt experience. No fewer than 70 percent of the reporters had worked in journalism for less than five years.

10. Seventy-eight percent of the judges were initially appointed to the bench, and of those, 90 percent had subsequently been reelected.

11. Whether there is a substantive difference between English and literature, I do not know. The reporters provided no further definition.

12. John W. C. Johnstone, Edward J. Slawski and William W. Bowman, *The News People* (Urbana: University of Illinois Press, 1976), pp. 201, 203.

13. Stephen Hess, *The Washington Reporters* (Washington, D.C.: Brookings Institution, 1981), pp. 156–57; Everette E. Dennis, "Another Look at Press Coverage of the Supreme Court," *Villanova Law Review* 20 (1974–75):791–92.

14. Hess, p. 156; Dennis, p. 792.

15. Sources weren't asked their ages, but the length of their experience indicates an age gap between them and reporters.

16. A screening question asked sources how frequently they were in the courtroom themselves. See appendix B, table B.2. Obviously, reporters may sometimes be present but go unrecognized.

17. The median was 27.5 percent, the mode 30 percent. The range was 0 to 93 percent.

18. This item wasn't particularly relevant to clerks, so it isn't surprising that so few are asked for such assistance.

19. A number of respondents of all types did write on the questionnaire that their responses assumed that public records were involved. Perhaps the questionnaire ought to have made that distinction, but unfortunately the pretesting did not indicate any potential problem.

20. Sources were also asked whether they would provide the same types of information to anyone, not just reporters. The vast majority said they would, although fewer attorneys than judges and clerks said they would. A number of respondents also penciled in such responses as "sometimes" or "depends." These responses were counted as neither yes nor no.

21. Of course, no comparison is possible across branches since these data were gathered only from judicial sources.

22. On the other hand, one public defender complained that "newspapers are scared to death of judges and fail to scrutinize their behavior as is done with other elected officials."

23. Reporters were asked to estimate what percentage of their information they obtained through interviewing, observation of court proceedings, documents, news releases and press conferences, and other sources. The averages were then averaged. In the case of documents, the median response was 47 percent, the mode 40 percent. Responses ranged from 0 to 90 percent.

24. The median was 27.5 percent, the mode 30 percent, and the range 0 to 93 percent.

25. The median was 19.8 percent, the mode 20 percent, the range 0 to 60 percent.

26. Less than 1 percent of the information came from news releases and news conferences. The median was 0.05 percent, the mode 0 percent, and the range 1 to 20 percent.

6

The Basis for Reporter-Source
Interaction

Chapter 5 examined the mechanics of judicial reporter-source interaction. This chapter focuses more specifically on why sources cooperate with reporters and what sources and reporters view as appropriate roles or functions for the press as it covers the trial courts. First, the survey data are presented and discussed; then this data and some of the data from chapter 5 are integrated and their implications considered.

WHY SOURCES COOPERATE

Sources were asked whether or not they cooperated—or would cooperate—with reporters for each of a list of reasons.[1] Some were related to what chapter 2 defined as "manipulative" publicity; some were related to more general publicity for the judiciary as an institution; some were related to relevant commodities other than publicity. Reporters were asked why they believed sources cooperated with them. If, as I have suggested, judicial sources don't need the press like sources in other branches of government, one wouldn't expect self-oriented, manipulative reasons to motivate many judicial sources. To the degree that they do, one would expect to see this slightly more among attorneys than among other sources. That is generally what the responses suggest, as tables 6.1 and 6.2 show. Consider the reasons for cooperating one by one.

It can be satisfying to see one's name in the newspaper. This would seem to be a self-oriented, if not manipulative, reason for cooperation. For an attorney, seeing one's name in the paper might mean that one's side in a legal matter is receiving useful attention; or it may provide publicity that helps build a name and reputation, and consequently a larger or more lucrative practice. Or a politically minded judge might see publicity as a

TABLE 6.1 Percentage of Sources Who Have Cooperated or Would Cooperate with Reporters for Various Reasons

Reason for Cooperating	Clerks	Judges	All Attys.	County Attys.	Public Defenders	Private Attys.
It can be satisfying to see one's name in the newspaper	3%	18%	18%	17%	14%	24%
Good newspaper reporting can build public support for judicial decisions	76	84	64	73	52	65
Publicity is important to a public official or attorney	3	25	9	8	8	13
The people have a right to know	55	80	50	74	37	38
Source welcomes chance to explain his/her actions or other court action	26	53	47	56	46	38
Through press, members of bar and bench can find out what source is doing	.....*	17	7	11	6	5
Reporter is competent and knowledgeable	38	48	41	35	43	44
Fairly or not, reporter or newspaper may be uncooperative, critical or hostile if source doesn't cooperate	11	16	15	24	11	8
Reporter may reciprocate and provide source with useful or interesting information	6	6	12	15	11	8
Source wants to avoid errors in stories	74	84	76	82	78	67
Publicity about a case might contribute to a just, correct result	.....†	.....‡	26	17	40	22
	n = 66	n = 134	n = 192	n = 66	n = 63	n = 63

* Clerks were instead asked whether they cooperated because they felt a legal responsibility to cooperate; 67% said they cooperated for this reason.
† Not asked of clerks.
‡ Not asked of judges.

TABLE 6.2 Percentage of Reporters Who Believe Sources Have Cooperated for Various Reasons*

Reason for Cooperating	Clerks	Judges	Prosecutors	Criminal Defense Attys.	Other Attys.	Number of Cases
Being asked makes sources feel important	30%	26%	35%	17%	17%	23
Sources believe they may benefit personally or professionally from publicity	4	44	57	48	30	23
Sources think publicity may influence the outcome of a case to their liking	5	5	18	36	27	22
Sources believe people have a right to know	35	78	39	22	22	23
Sources welcome chance to explain themselves or an occurrence in court	22	78	70	61	30	23
Sources believe press can provide means by which their colleagues can find out what they are doing	0	13	17	30	17	23
Sources believe good reporting can build public support for judicial decisions	9	64	32	9	9	22
Sources consider the reporter to be competent and knowledgeable	44	61	52	30	35	23
Sources fear that reporter or newspaper may be uncooperative, critical or hostile if they don't cooperate	18	9	18	27	18	23
Sources believe reporter may reciprocate and provide them with interesting or useful information	5	5	27	18	9	22
Sources wish to avoid errors in stories	61	83	70	57	30	23
Sources feel legal responsibility to cooperate (e.g., because of open records laws)	57	52	74	39	13	23

* Reporters were not asked to distinguish federal from state sources.

political asset. Yet very few sources cited this reason, nor did many report-ers believe sources cooperate because being asked makes them feel important.[2] Although more judges and attorneys than clerks cited this reason, the numbers were still small; and that is no surprise.

Good newspaper reporting can build public support for judicial decisions. This reason suggests publicity as a motive, but publicity more for the judicial system as an institution than for strictly personal, manipulative reasons. Therefore, it isn't surprising to see the number of sources who cited this reason. One would expect judges especially to cooperate for this reason since they are the prime decision-makers, and the data bear this out. The reporters seem to underestimate this motive. Perhaps they are simply reluctant to ascribe benign motives to sources; but if the sources meant what they said, reporters might consider appealing to such motives when seeking source cooperation.

Publicity is important to a public official or attorney. This reason sug-gests a manipulative motive, publicity for personal gain. Again, few sources cited it. The fact that notably more judges than other sources cited it may reflect their elective status or desire for higher appointment, but even so, few judges cited the reason. The reporters apparently see the situation differently, although they were responding to a statement that put the reason in blunter language. Of course, once again just a few sources cooperating for this reason could have inflated the reporters' re-sponse, so the sources' own response may be the more valid measure.

The people have a "right to know." This is a nonpublicity reason in the sense that the need is the public's rather than the source's or the judicial system's. Many sources cited this reason, particularly judges and county attorneys. Perhaps this is because as elected officials they feel more re-sponsibility to the public. Perhaps county attorneys also inherently benefit from most disclosure because publicity in criminal cases is likely to benefit the prosecution. Since clerks are the custodians of documents which are legally public records, one might expect more clerks to cooperate be-cause of a right to know, but barely half of them do. That, coupled with the fact that only two-thirds of the clerks said they cooperated because they felt a legal responsibility to, may suggest that clerks are hardly the most disclosure-oriented sources.[3] Why this should be is unclear, but re-porters apparently perceived it, too. Note that reporters generally under-estimated sources' right-to-know motive, and this may again reflect a reluctance to assume the best about source motives.

I welcome a chance to explain myself or something which happened in court. This statement seems to suggest publicity for benign reasons. However, it could also provide an attorney with an opportunity to obtain more publicity for his or her side in a case, thus giving attorneys a ma-nipulative reason to cooperate. As elected officials, judges may also see practical political value in explaining themselves to voters. But assuming that the motive is primarily nonmanipulative, the fact that about half the judges and attorneys cited it is not surprising. The similarity between judges and county attorneys may reflect feelings of obligation as elected officials to explain themselves to the public. Judges in particular are in a good position to explain court action for altruistic reasons. Besides, judges are expected to explain the reasons for their decisions; were this not the case, the case reporters would be thin volumes indeed. On the other hand, public defenders and other attorneys might consider publicity a greater risk than advantage and thus refrain from going beyond the public record. The low number of clerks citing this reason may simply reflect that they don't do much that requires an explanation.

By means of the press, other members of the bench and bar can find out what I am doing. This reason was not presented to clerks because it is inapplicable to them. But it was presented to judges and attorneys because one of the premises suggested in chapter 2 was that judicial sources do not need the press as a communication link among themselves. The response supports this clearly.

The reporter is competent and knowledgeable. This is a nonpublicity reason. Considering bench and bar complaints about incompetent reporters, it is surprising that more sources didn't cite reporter competence as a reason for cooperating. Perhaps it is because sources believe there are so few competent reporters. That is, if one thinks that all reporters are incompetent, one might never cooperate with a competent one because one might never meet a competent one. Still, the question asked sources whether they either had cooperated or *would* cooperate for these reasons. Yet another possibility is that some sources may feel threatened by a truly competent court reporter since such a reporter could be harder for a source to control. In any case, it would seem that sources can't have it both ways, complaining about the press and yet not necessarily being willing to cooperate with a truly competent reporter.

Fairly or not, the reporter or newspaper may be uncooperative, critical or hostile if I don't cooperate. If, as I suggested, judicial sources have relatively little personal need for the press, they shouldn't have much reason to fear a hostile or uncooperative reporter or newspaper. The results—both from sources and reporters—corroborate this. The sources citing this reason most often were the county attorneys. Perhaps as elected officials they feel they have the most to lose, but judges were not equally concerned. Perhaps it is just that county attorneys have the most contact with reporters and therefore might consider reporter hostility to be a more significant problem. Even so, less than 1 county attorney in 4 cited this reason.

The reporter may reciprocate and provide me with interesting or useful information. If, in fact, judicial sources have little need for information reporters may have, this should not be a major motive for cooperation. Once again, the results support this. More attorneys than judges or clerks did cite this reason, and perhaps it is because they might be able to make more practical use of such information. Or perhaps attorneys are somewhat more isolated. But to reiterate: Very few sources or reporters cited this reason.

I want to avoid errors in newspaper stories. Given complaints about inaccurate court reporting, one would expect this to be a major reason for source cooperation, and apparently such is the case. The reporters seem to have underestimated the importance of this reason. Perhaps that is because reporters have relatively little contact with some source types. But it may be that reporters simply do not perceive inaccuracy to be a major problem—at least not to the degree that sources do. Reporters may do well to remember how important a motive for cooperation this is to sources.

Publicity about a case might contribute to a just, correct result. This would appear to be a manipulative reason, one which implies involving publicity in the decision-making process. Judges and clerks were not given this alternative; overall, few attorneys cited it. And when reporters were asked baldly whether sources cooperate because they think publicity may influence the outcome of a case to their liking, few so indicated. The fact that more reporters thought attorneys, as opposed to clerks and judges, cooperated for this reason is consistent with the expectation that attorneys are the judicial sources most likely to desire publicity for manipulative reasons. The defense attorneys stand out in both reporter and source responses. Perhaps this is not only because they wish to do everything possible for clients, but because the ordinary run of publicity tends otherwise to favor the prosecution.

To summarize, the evidence on why sources cooperate does indicate that manipulative publicity sought for personal reasons is not a major motivation for sources, nor is a desire to obtain information from reporters or fear of the press. Cooperation is based more on the perceived value of publicity for the judicial system, the public's right to know and a desire for accuracy. Such results support the idea that the press's role in the judicial branch is more circumscribed than its role in other branches, that consequently reporter-source relations may be affected and that sources may be in a more powerful position than reporters.

How much attention, then, do sources pay to the media? Ninety-one percent of the clerks, 91 percent of the judges,[4] 94 percent of county attorneys, 98 percent of public defenders and 71 percent of private attorneys said they generally read newspaper accounts of cases they handle, or, in the case of clerks, cases of which they have firsthand knowledge.

The rationale laid out in chapter 2 suggests that judicial sources will not rely heavily on the press for useful information about judicial action, and sources' responses provide some support for this. Between a fourth and a third of all judicial sources said they do not rely on the press at all for such information, while less than 15 percent of them said they rely on the press a great deal for such information.

Sources rely more on the media as indicators of the public image of local courts. More than 80 percent of all source types said they rely on the media either some or a great deal for this purpose. In light of the image problems experienced by the judiciary, it isn't surprising that sources would be image-conscious. Whether newspapers are a particularly good indication of public image is another question. In any case, such use of the press seems to be more system-oriented or institution-oriented than individual-oriented, and that is consistent with what one would expect of judicial sources.

PRESS ROLES AND SOURCE ROLES

To get a more direct indication of what kind of role judicial sources and reporters believe is appropriate for the press as it covers trial courts, both groups were asked to react to a series of role-oriented statements. The results have implications for the judicial news-making process. And from the response, we can see more fundamentally what sources and reporters agree and disagree about.

The statements were in part designed to see how active or passive a role would be conceded to the press. From a source's standpoint, a passive press role is a more benign, cooperative one; an active role implies more press probing and aggressiveness. Some of the statements also imply that the press should provide publicity that is educational, others imply more analytical publicity and others imply that the press should defer to the judiciary. How sources and reporters react to these statements should suggest something about their orientations toward information dissemination.

For each statement, respondents were asked to react on a scale of strongly agree, agree, neither agree nor disagree, disagree, or strongly disagree; a score of 5 corresponds to strongly agree, 1 to strongly disagree. Medians were computed for each respondent-type's response to each statement. Table 6.3 shows the results. It is worth considering the statements individually.

The press should confine itself primarily to reporting the facts of court cases as they unfold in public records and proceedings. This statement suggests a fairly passive role for the press, and obviously the sources would like to see such a press orientation, while the reporters would not.

Such fundamental source-reporter disagreement may be a potential source of tension.

The press should provide as objectively factual an account of court action as is humanly possible. Not surprisingly, most respondents agreed with this statement more intensely than with the previous statement. From the sources' standpoint, the statement probably implies fair coverage; for the reporters, it reflects one of journalism's fundamental canons. One reason for the stronger agreement with this statement may be that being objective does not inherently restrict one to using public records and proceedings, but it does imply quality coverage. In any case, the response suggests that regardless of how active or passive respondents believe the press should be, they agree about the value of objectivity.

It is important for the press to provide readers with useful information about the judicial branch of government. Since chapter 2 suggested that judicial sources would generally be "informers" or "educators" who think highly of the public's need for information, the across-the-board agreement with this statement is understandable. It doesn't necessarily suggest either a strongly active or passive press role, so sources can be comfortable with it; so can reporters, since the press frequently claims this function as one of its *raisons d'être*. The judges' strong agreement may indicate that, as primary representatives and symbols of the judicial branch, they feel a strong institutional interest in the public having such information. Clearly, sources and reporters agree on this press role.

The press should continuously attempt to educate the public about the judicial process and the role of the judiciary. Since this function is public-oriented and judicial institution-oriented, respondents' agreement with it is understandable. Reporters do appear more willing to assume this educational role than sources might like, and this may be because it implies at least a slightly more active press. Again, reporters and sources generally agree about the appropriateness of this press function.

The press should do as much as possible to avoid conflict with the judicial branch of government. How does the press avoid conflict? Most easily by being cautious, sticking to the facts as presented in public records and public proceedings, and being highly cognizant of remaining as neutral as possible. In other words, this statement implies a passive, cooperative, deferent press. What is particularly interesting is the sources' reactions to this press posture—more specifically, their tendency to be neutral and even disagree with it. Understandably, the reporters reacted negatively to such a passive orientation, but how can we understand the judges and attorneys? And why should the clerks be a clear exception? One possibility is that legal training sensitizes judges and attorneys more to the constitutional position of the press. And judges and attorneys are in effect socialized to value at least controlled conflict. The nature of their trade is

TABLE 6.3 Median Rating Given by Sources and Reporters to Possible Press Roles*

Role of Press	Clerks	Judges	All Attys.	County Attys.	Public Defenders	Private Attys.	Reporters
The press should confine itself primarily to reporting the facts of court cases as they unfold in public records and proceedings	4 (65)†	4 (133)	4 (189)	4 (64)	4 (63)	4 (62)	2 (24)
The press should provide as objectively factual an account of court action as is humanly possible	4 (65)	5 (135)	5 (189)	5 (65)	5 (63)	5 (61)	5 (23)
It is important for the press to provide readers with useful information about the judicial branch of government	4 (65)	5 (135)	4 (189)	4 (64)	4 (63)	4 (62)	4.5 (24)
The press should continuously attempt to educate the public about the judicial process and the role of the judiciary	4 (64)	4 (134)	4 (189)	4 (64)	4 (63)	4 (62)	5 (24)
The press should do as much as possible to avoid conflict with the judicial branch of government	4 (63)	3 (134)	3 (186)	3 (64)	3 (62)	2.5 (60)	2 (24)

In their stories, it often can be important for news reporters to interpret and/or analyze court action for readers	2 (65)	3 (135)	3 (190)	2 (65)	4 (63)	4 (62)	4 (24)
The press should be a watchdog over the courts and their officials and officers	2 (64)	3 (134)	4 (189)	4 (65)	4 (62)	4 (62)	5 (24)
Reporters should always consider that what they write can positively or negatively affect the public image of the local trial courts	4 (64)	4 (134)	4 (187)	4 (65)	4 (63)	4 (59)	2 (23)
It is legitimate for newspaper reporters to use their court stories to point out what they perceive to be flaws and problems in the local courts and to suggest possible solutions	2 (61)	4 (134)	4 (187)	4 (65)	4 (63)	4 (59)	4 (23)

* Respondents rated each press role on a 5-point scale with 1 corresponding to "strongly disagree"; 2 to "disagree"; 3 to "neither agree nor disagree"; 4 to "agree"; and 5 to "strongly agree."

† Number in parentheses indicates number of respondents on which median is based.

adversarial; why should they shy away from conflict with the press? Overall, the response to this statement is striking because it suggests that most judicial sources do not regard disagreement with the press as fundamentally evil.

In their stories, it often can be important for news reporters to analyze court action for readers. This suggests a more active role for the press, and reporter-source disagreement about it may indicate a basis for press-court conflict. Obviously, reporters feel this function is more appropriate than do the majority of sources. Why is the disagreement especially sharp between reporters and clerks and county attorneys? Perhaps the clerks' training and background leads them to this position relative to judges and most attorneys. But what of the county attorneys? It may simply be that they have the most to lose as the press begins to wander away from simple recitation of facts from documents and proceedings, since such basic information is frequently inherently favorable to the prosecution. Similar reasoning may explain why public defenders and private attorneys agreed with the statement. A more active press may be more useful to them.

The press should be a watchdog over the courts and their officials and officers. Again, there is a clear difference between the reporters and sources on a statement that implies an active, analytical press role. But equally noteworthy is how many sources are willing to deem this role appropriate. That is consistent with the argument that judicial sources will generally be "informers" or "educators" with a public orientation. But the clerks continue to puzzle. Perhaps they feel more threatened by this active role; perhaps the difference is related to their backgrounds and ministerial duties.

Reporters should always consider that what they write can positively or negatively affect the public image of the local trial courts. This item clearly discriminated reporters and sources, and suggests an obvious basis for disagreement and potential conflict. The sources' response indicates that they have considerable solicitude for their institution. Taken together with sources' positions on other statements, this response suggests some ambivalence; that is, it may be acceptable for the press to be somewhat watchful and analytical, but it should do so in the best interest of the judiciary.

It is legitimate for newspaper reporters to use their court stories to point out what they perceive to be flaws and problems in the local courts and to suggest possible solutions. Perhaps the most striking result here is the agreement among reporters, judges and attorneys, even though this statement suggests an active, analytical role for the press. The response is consistent with the idea that judicial sources are generally not promoters. The anomaly again is the clerks' response, which is consistent with their apparent unwillingness to grant the press any kind of active role.

To summarize, then, we can say that reporters and sources agree to a surprising degree on what roles and functions are appropriate for the press as it covers trial courts. Both groups are willing to see the press as an educator and, to a degree, as an interpreter and critic of trial court activity. They agree on the value of objective reporting, and they agree that the press should at least not defer to the judiciary by doing as much as possible to avoid conflict. On the other hand, the sources appear to prefer a more passive press than do the reporters, and therein lies potential for reporter-source friction. That is, as reporters move toward a participant orientation and away from the neutral, they put more distance between themselves and sources. Such distance could constrict the flow of information from the judiciary, particularly if sources have relatively little incentive to cooperate anyway.

The response to the role statements also has implications for source role types—informer, educator and promoter. The responses were generally consistent with the view that judicial sources tend to be informers and educators. But the clerks were enigmatic. Their view of appropriate activity by the press is conservative. Perhaps this is a function of nonlegal backgrounds. Perhaps clerks feel loyalty to their judges to the point of becoming overprotective. They may believe their opinions mirror judges'; if so, they are often wrong.[5]

Still, there is no compelling reason to conclude that clerks must be "promoter" sources. That possibility is discounted if we consider other evidence bearing on role types. For example, the .data on the kind of information sources have provided or would provide show generally that attorneys are more willing than clerks and judges to provide assistance such as opinions and speculation, story suggestions and help in determining newsworthiness. That is, attorneys appear more active in trying to shape coverage, something we might expect of promoters. Or if we consider the reasons for which sources will cooperate, very few clerks cited the reasons that implied more manipulative motives. In fact, as expected, none of the sources showed consistent, strong signs of being "promoters" who put self-interest clearly over public interest. The only source type to show even slight indication of being a "promoter" was the attorneys, particularly the county attorneys. But as I have said before, this is not surprising. County attorneys may be the most politically ambitious of the sources. They may have the most to gain from the right publicity. But few of even these sources showed "promoter" inclinations.

What all this implies for the news-making process is that judicial source-reporter relations should be generally compatible—relatively free of conflict. If there is conflict, one would expect it most likely to involve attorneys, especially county attorneys.[6] That such is the case is supported by table 6.4, which shows how often sources openly disagree with journalists about court coverage.

TABLE 6.4   Percentage of Sources Indicating Frequency of Open Disagreement with Reporters or Editors*

Source Type	**Frequency of Disagreement**				Total[†]	Number of Cases
	Never	Rarely	Occasionally	Frequently		
Clerks	53%	35%	11%	2%	101%	66%
Judges	38	40	17	5	100	134
All attorneys	42	27	27	4	100	191
County attorneys	27	33	32	8	100	66
Public defenders	40	29	29	3	101	63
Private attorneys	61	18	19	2	100	62

* The exact question was, "About how often have you and a local newspaper reporter or editor openly disagreed (e.g., by phone, in person or by letter) over the way some court action has been covered?"
[†] Some totals do not equal 100% due to rounding.

IMPLICATIONS

Chapter 2 suggested that the press would play a different role in its relationship with the judicial branch than with other branches of government, that sources in the judicial branch would use the press differently than sources in other branches. Data gathered from the sources and presented in the past two chapters seem to support this expectation.

For example, if we consider in a broader sense the value that judicial sources place on publicity per se, a reasonable conclusion is that they value it relatively little. Asked whether they cooperated with reporters because it was satisfying to see their names in print, few sources agreed. Asked whether they cooperated because publicity was important to them, few sources agreed. More sources said they cooperated because publicity might build public support for judicial decisions, but such publicity is generally post-decision rather than predecision publicity and institutional more than personal. Unlike other branches of government, the judiciary has no obvious way of building public support before a decision. Another finding was that relatively few attorney sources said they will cooperate with reporters because publicity could contribute to a just, correct result. Clearly, this does not suggest that sources place a high value on the use of publicity to attain desired ends. Of course, there are ethical reasons why judicial sources may not feel at liberty to use publicity this way even if they want to, but that only suggests yet another reason why the press-source relationship is different in the judicial branch.

Another indicator of the value placed on publicity by judicial sources is the low number who will provide a reporter with opinion or speculation about a case. Of course, this finding is not particularly surprising, since some comment might be considered a violation of professional ethics. Nevertheless, this finding supports the assumption that there is a different relationship between the press and sources in the judicial branch. More judicial sources are willing to suggest possible stories. But with the exception of the county attorneys, the number is less than half. This certainly contrasts with many other agencies of government which not only constantly suggest stories but provide an unending flow of already written ones in the form of publicity releases. There is no real public relations machinery in place in the trial courts; if stories are to be suggested, they are to be suggested by sources. And if less than half the sources are willing to do this, the flow of story ideas must be constricted.

This finding and conclusion are reinforced by the evidence from reporters that news conferences and press releases are virtually nonexistent as sources of judicial news and by the low number of judicial sources who say they have ever approached a local newspaper reporter with unsolicited information. Once again, the implication is that the judiciary does not place a high value on publicity—at least not high enough to pursue it more actively. It is true that the reporters indicated having received a considerable number of tips from judicial sources. But this does not necessarily contradict the sources' response since it is unknown how many sources were providing tips to reporters. Further, there were far fewer reporters than sources in the survey.

Chapter 2 noted that several studies of other branches of government have concluded that the press plays a role in helping sources communicate with each other and in carrying bits of information from one source to another both privately and in print. I suggested there that this was not likely to be the case in the judiciary, and the evidence was supportive. And sources indicated very little fear of reporter or newspaper hostility. Finally, relatively few sources reported relying a great deal on the news media for useful information about judicial decisions. What this suggests, of course, is that the trial courts simply don't need the press the way other branches of government might, that the courts have relatively little need for the press's prime commodity. Indeed, if the sources indicated that they used the press for anything, it was as an indicator of the courts' public image.

But if the courts appear relatively indifferent to the press, the press seems to return the favor. The vast majority of reporters have duties in addition to court coverage and spend very little time covering courts per se. Courts are generally covered by young and inexperienced reporters who have no legal training. The tremendous pressure of time would seem to force them to gather court news in the most efficient way possible; there would appear to be little time to cultivate a wide range of sources, much less to hassle endlessly with those who tend not to cooperate. Since so many judicial sources appear to be unaggressive in contacting reporters and since reporters must work quickly, it is logical for reporters to gravitate toward sources who are cooperative and generally easy to contact. This suggests that any source in the judiciary who is not only accessible and cooperative but may actually seek out a reporter will receive considerable attention and could have a disproportionate influence on court news. This may explain why both sources' and reporters' surveys suggest that prosecuting attorneys are very important in the news-making process. They are accessible, they have a great deal of information that reporters apparently want and need, and they are elected officials who clearly feel some responsibility to communicate their activities to the public. And because much of the information that surfaces at least early in the criminal court process favors prosecution over defense, publicity is desirable for the prosecution. No wonder reporters rely on county attorneys so heavily,[7] and no wonder that upsets public defenders.

In light of all this, what is interesting is that, in general, more judicial sources of all types are willing to provide various types of information to reporters than are asked. This only confirms that these sources are relatively unaggressive and that reporters might be the same. This must inevitably constrict information flow out of the judicial system. What appears to exist, therefore, is a branch of government in which sources do not need the press for the same reasons as sources in other branches; yet judicial sources would apparently like more coverage and better coverage, particularly coverage which would increase public understanding of the courts; but the same sources are relatively unwilling to take the initiative in contacting reporters and editors to obtain such coverage. The reason may be simply that the judicial branch is less overtly political than other branches; that, consequently, sources' reasons for cooperating are more abstract than personally profitable; and that therefore the most concrete incentives for sources to be aggressive are generally absent, or when they are present, judicial and professional ethics tend to moderate or temper them.

This research also sheds light on reasons why bench and bar have been so critical of the press. It is understandable that sources—or potential sources—will be critical when the press employs so few resources to cover their branch of government. Criticism is understandable when sources highly trained in a technical and precision-oriented profession are confronted with often inexperienced reporters with little technical training who must write for a lay audience.[8] It is understandable that conflict might arise when reporters' concept of press role and function is a more active one than that of sources. And the situation is probably exacerbated in a system in which sources appear not to need or want many of the commodities that reporters can offer.

On the other hand, it is understandable that reporters with so little time to devote to judicial coverage can be in turn frustrated by a system which often seems utterly unconscious of time. Reporters with limited time to work must of necessity shy away from long stints in the courtroom which can be relatively unproductive or interrupted by seemingly endless delay. It is understandable—perhaps inevitable—that such reporters will gravitate toward the most cooperative sources. And when those sources are documents, they are frequently one-sided by definition. When those cooperative sources are attorneys, the information they provide may well be less than objective and balanced. But other sources might do more to take the initiative themselves. Also, a certain amount of complaining must originate from sources who themselves are not in a position to be objective.

Of course, errors in newspaper court stories are inexcusable, but they are understandable. Yet it is striking that reporters say that they find most judicial sources to be cooperative or very cooperative, and that when all sources are combined, three-fourths say they have never or only rarely openly disagreed with a local reporter or editor about court coverage.

Perhaps what this suggests is that so far as the bulk of routine court coverage goes, the press and trial courts get along quite well and that the unusual cases involving egregious conduct on one side or the other are those that stimulate the most complaints. If this is not the case—and if the sources meant it when they indicated that they have little fear of newspaper hostility or criticism—then both sides would be better served by a greater willingness to disagree openly in a civilized manner.

SUMMARY AND CONCLUSIONS

The preceding two chapters reported the results of a survey of judges, court clerks, attorneys and daily newspaper court reporters in Minnesota. The objective was to gather data on reporter-source interaction in state trial courts, on why sources cooperate and what roles they feel are appropriate for the press.

In effect, this was a pilot case study of news making in one state court system. I cannot claim that the results and conclusions are generalizable to all state court systems or to the federal court system. On the other hand, there would seem to be no patently obvious reason why similar results should not be obtained in many other state court systems.

Notes

1. An open-ended category was also provided but produced few responses.
2. This reason, however, may represent a slightly different dimension.
3. This orientation may also be reflected in the fact that 41 percent of the clerks have no formal or informal office policy on cooperation with the news media.

4. The percentage was the same for judges regardless of whether the case was a jury case or an action only before the judge.

5. This possibility was suggested to me by a judge during a discussion of the results.

6. All of this assumes that few, if any, reporters are "prescribers." The reporters' reaction to the press-role statements suggests that this is so. That would be consistent with Stanga's findings. See chapter 2, p. 18.

7. Much of the same logic would apply to law enforcement sources, making it understandable why reporters make so much use of them. But they are outside the scope of this study.

8. It is not surprising, therefore, that more than twice as many clerks as any other type of source specifically said they had no complaints about the press. Their background and training probably resembles reporters more than other judicial sources in the sense that they are more like laymen themselves.

7

Conclusions and Recommendations

The preceding four chapters examined the routine news-making process in trial courts by using historical, observational and survey research. This chapter briefly synthesizes the findings of those chapterrs, offers some suggestions to judicial sources and journalists and suggests directions for further research.

AN OVERVIEW

Historical study disclosed that reporting of American trial courts is virtually as old as American newspapers themselves, that trial courts did receive considerable coverage throughout the eighteenth century and that eighteenth-century newspapers did not hesitate to publicize even the most distasteful offenses. The reporting was concise, straightforward and occasionally moralistic. It focused on criminal cases. Two major changes occurred in the nineteenth century. First, reporters became more active newsgatherers in the courts, attended myriad court proceedings and ultimately moved outside the courtroom to interview aggressively participants in the judicial process.[1] Second, although the quantitative bulk of trial court reporting was verbatim stenography, reporters began to add colorful description of the scenes and people they observed in the courtroom. As the twentieth century arrived, reporters were relying much less on verbatim reporting and stories were written much as they are today.

These findings challenge, at least in part, the common interpretation that eighteenth-century American newspapers generally ignored local news. Clearly, local courts were not ignored as news sources. I certainly found more coverage than the secondary historical sources had led me to expect. Further, even during the penny press era and again in the yellow

journalism period, the bulk of trial court reporting was quite objective—
at least to the degree that objectivity is defined as correspondence between a court proceeding and the report of the proceeding. Obviously,
this was due largely to the stenographic approach used. The research suggests, therefore, that when trial court reporting is examined by itself, it is
a mistake to assume that the colorful police court reporting of the mid-
1830s was representative of court reporting generally. It is equally a mistake to assume that the egregious sensationalism of the yellow journalism
era was representative of trial court reporting generally.

Historical research also illustrates how painstakingly slowly change
has come in trial court reporting. One of the most striking findings was
how little reporting changed during the two centuries studied. From 1704
until the second decade of the nineteenth century, change was virtually
undetectable in terms of writing style, story selection, use of sources and
news-gathering technique. However, noticeable change occurred beginning in the 1820s, change which corresponded with the appearance of the
first full-time reporters. Coverage became more exhaustive, lengthy,
embellished and colorful. Where the bulk of court reporting from the
preceding century had been concise summary, much of the new court reporting was detailed and verbatim. Newsgatherers were as much steno-
graphers as journalists. Police court reporting notwithstanding, it was the
last half of the nineteenth century before movement away from the strictly verbatim reporting began and interviewing emerged as a common
news-gathering technique. And it was the last quarter of the nineteenth
century that saw much court reporting take the form in which it still
appears. In one sense, the process had come full circle: from concise summary of court action in the eighteenth century, to exhaustive (if not ex-
hausting) verbatim coverage through most of the nineteenth century,
back to greater use of summary, although not nearly as concise as that of
the eighteenth century.

Comparison is profitable at this point with court reporting in the
twentieth century. Unquestionably, stenographic, verbatim reporting has
disappeared. In general, so have the colorful and descriptive but highly
subjective judgmental statements reporters themselves frequently employed to introduce the verbatim portions of their stories or which they
would insert unashamedly into a nonverbatim account. Thus, in one respect, trial court reporting now may be less fair and objective than that of
the nineteenth century simply because it no longer leans heavily on the
verbatim record. In another respect, however, reporting today is more
objective if by that we mean that it generally lacks blatantly judgmental
statements by reporters.[2] This change is particularly noteworthy since it
may suggest that the press has become more responsive to the fair trial
rights of litigants, especially criminal defendants. Nor should this be surprising, since, at least so far as the states are concerned, it has only been
in the twentieth century that federal courts have found the states to be

bound by the provisions of the Bill of Rights.[3] As chapter 3 pointed out, there may have been relatively little emphasis on defendants' rights in the eighteenth and nineteenth centuries. Newspaper reporting certainly has not developed in a vacuum; it has been influenced by other forces in society.

In any case, it seems reasonable—based on historical comparison—to suggest that at least in fair trial terms, the newspaper press today is generally more responsible than it has ever been. Perhaps the press could avoid disagreement with bench and bar if it still reported court cases verbatim, but that is really not journalism at all; it is merely stenography, involving no news judgment, no intellectual work, no summarizing, no selection or organization of material, no particular attention to audience and certainly no creative activity. To whatever degree reporters attempt to interpret and explain, or even merely to summarize what happens in court, to that degree the potential for conflict with the judiciary increases.

A comparison of historical evidence with the observational and survey evidence presented in chapters 4, 5, and 6 suggests that reporters have remained oriented strongly toward spot news about cases, particularly criminal cases. It was the latter half of the nineteenth century before stories about the judicial system or broader legal issues first appeared. Even then they were not common. The same is true today. This further suggests that news values have not changed significantly so far as court news is concerned for nearly two centuries. One might even argue that court coverage today is less exhaustive than it was a century ago. There is some evidence that nineteenth-century newspapers were giving at least some ink to nearly every local court case and were publishing daily court calenders. This suggests that members of the legal profession may have been an important audience in those days. If so, the press may then have been an important communication channel providing attorneys and perhaps even judges with needed information.[4] That is no longer the case, as the survey research illustrates. In effect, then, it may be that one reason for twentieth-century press-court conflict is that there is less of a symbiotic relationship between press and judiciary than in the past.

This in turn has several implications—implications suggested by the observational and survey research. First, although a desire for publicity—particularly manipulative publicity in the case of some sources—remains a motivating factor for judicial sources, they may well be more reluctant now than before to seek publicity for such reasons. This is because sources indicate little need for the press as an intrajudicial communication link, because professional ethics undoubtedly exert some restraint on the cooperation of sources generally and because there is more sensitivity today to defendants' rights. The last of these reasons may explain why press interviews with criminal defendants are more rare now than in the past. Even if cooperation for blatantly manipulative reasons has decreased, it is not surprising to find—as the survey did—that many sources cooperate for the more general publicity purpose of enhancing public understanding of the judicial system and of building support for judicial decisions. Obviously, it is impossible to know how many sources cooperated for this reason two centuries ago, but we know that they do so now.

Assuming that judicial sources in fact do need reporters less today than a century ago, the balance of power between the groups ought to have been affected, with reporters being the losers. At first, this might not seem particularly important since judicial proceedings and records are open to the press and public; but as noted before, reporters are faced with serious time problems. They need help in determining how to use this scarce resource, in filling in details about action they cannot observe and, of course, in fleshing out stories about the system itself. Furthermore, courts handle more cases and more complex cases than ever before, making reporters' jobs even more difficult. Huge caseloads covered by few reporters means, as the observational study illustrated, coverage that is relatively chancy. That is, press attention may be determined to a significant degree simply by source tips, irrespective of the relative importance of the information involved vis-à-vis all potentially available court information.[5] Thus to the degree that reporters need sources to help them solve their time problems, they become vulnerable to sources, particularly those who are cooperative and aggressive in initiating and encouraging contact. Obviously, this can lead to one-sided coverage, or at least it can skew coverage in directions that might not be taken if reporters had the time and resources to assure their independence. Indeed, what some in the judicial branch might perceive as inadequate performance by the press may be the inevitable result of just this situation.

Furthermore, reporters' need for help in determining what to cover (and thus how to best invest their limited time) is also met by looking at what has been covered before. This concurrently decreases the amount of "new" material coming out of the judiciary. Meanwhile, reporters are further disadvantaged since they generally lack the legal expertise which would give them more independence from sources in judging the significance of potential stories. Thus one inescapable conclusion of this study must be that a tremendous amount of potentially newsworthy material is lost within the court system, and some of that material may be more important than that which is reported.

I do not want to suggest that reporters are powerless. They can and do ignore some source initiatives; they can and do consider sources' motives; they can and do initiate contact with sources; they can and do independently decide to cover a case or initiate a feature story idea; they can and do have independent access to court documents and proceedings; they can and do—consciously or not—offer sources a channel for publicity; and they can and do offer sources such exchange commodities as friendship, trust and enjoyable social contact. Finally, they can—and I believe they unconsciously or consciously do—use objectivity itself to maintain some independence from sources.

Overall, however, sources in the trial courts seem to hold more power than reporters, if for no other reason than the fact that they have relatively little need for the press's prime commodity—publicity. Yet most sources seem generally uninterested in aggressively using that power. Those who do use it appear to receive attention.

In sum, the results suggest that exchange behavior does exist between reporters and sources in trial courts, that trial court news making, like news making elsewhere, is a sociopolitical process, and that judicial sources do act in role types. But the findings also demonstrate that there may indeed be important differences between reporter-source relationships in the trial courts and reporter-source relationships in other branches of government since manipulative publicity is not a strong motivation for source cooperation in the trial courts.

SUGGESTIONS

The results of this research suggest that judicial sources have a considerable opportunity to be more aggressive in initiating contact with reporters. One way to improve coverage might be to increase such contact and cooperation within the bounds of professional ethics. Ideally, such an approach should not be demanding or always self-serving; but the point is that reporters' time constraints may put them in a situation where they need sources' assistance but are otherwise unable to substantially widen contacts on their own.

Sources can't have it both ways: they cannot blithely complain about poor or one-sided coverage but decline to help reporters. I suspect that frequently complaints about one-sidedness are traceable to some sources being more cooperative than others. Clearly, reporters are not blameless in such situations, but neither are sources; attorneys and judges ought at least to focus more criticism on the inappropriate behavior of their colleagues.

One of the interesting findings of this study was that in many respects judges and attorneys were more alike than judges and clerks or attorneys and clerks. Judges and attorneys were surprisingly willing to grant the press an active role in covering the judiciary; clerks preferred a more passive role for the press. This suggests that the press may find more of a reservoir of goodwill and understanding amongst bench and bar than it might expect.

Sources' attitudes about the press may also have implications for their official actions affecting the press. Perhaps in a larger sense, judges' and attorneys' willingness to grant an active role to the press—to the degree that it reflects a basic sensitivity to the value of a free press—makes them relatively reluctant to try to restrict the press. For example, were it not for these attitudes, such impingements on freedom of the press as closing judicial proceedings to the press and public might be far more common. Of course, it is one thing to concede an active role to the press in the abstract, but quite another when such a role conflicts with a case one is handling. Nevertheless, at least at the abstract level the attitudes are there.

One way to anticipate and perhaps defuse unproductive conflict with the press might be for law schools to build on sources' attitudes by bringing journalism professors and working reporters into the classroom. This would provide an early opportunity for contact, exchange of ideas and, with luck, move the sides closer to mutual understanding. Such contact inside the law school should be frequent. It might be handled through a seminar mechanism, but it might well be built into classes to which press coverage of cases is especially relevant. In other words, there may be as great a need for judicial sources to learn about the press as there is for the press to learn more about the judiciary.

There are indications that such a need is beginning to be recognized. Judge Donald R. Fretz of California has prepared a series of texts for the National College of the State Judiciary that provide fundamental information and advice to judicial sources about dealing with the news media.[6] The American Bar Association has prepared a public relations guide for state and local bar associations that deals in part with news media relations.[7] And in Minnesota, the state supreme court information office has published an 89-page guidebook for clerks, judges and other court personnel on how to share information with the public.[8]

Clerks occupy a somewhat different position than judges and attorneys since their duties are primarily administrative. But they occupy a crucial position for reporters seeking access to court records and information. Needless conflict between them and reporters can severely constrict information flow from the trial courts. The fact that clerks prefer a passive role for the press suggests that the potential for conflict may be great. Again, contact between groups outside of the working environment to discuss such differences and better understand each other's jobs and problems would be fruitful. This might also lead more clerks to adopt some type of policy on information release and access to records which all office personnel could follow, thus making the accessibility of records predictable. At minimum, however, such policy should follow common and statute law on open records.

It is too easy and probably quixotic to suggest that newspapers give reporters more time and resources to cover trial courts. But even without such a commitment, there is room for change. For example, newspapers and reporters might rethink their predominant orientation to coverage of criminal cases and to coverage of the trial courts as basically spot news factories. Certainly, criminal cases are important, but are they as inherently important as coverage seems to assume? Or are they in part covered more because it is easier for reporters and editors without legal expertise to apply their news judgment to them than to civil cases the significance of which is more obtuse? Are criminal cases really generally more worthy of coverage because they invoke the power of the state, while civil cases are essentially disputes between private individuals? Or is that analysis far too simplistic?

Editors and reporters might consider trading some of the time spent on coverage of routine spot news in the trial courts for time devoted to stories covering the courts as an institution and to stories examining broader legal issues and their implications at the local level. The press frequently justifies its need for access to specific judicial proceedings and documents on grounds that such continuing public scrutiny is essential to ensuring a responsible judiciary. But might such scrutiny not be even better achieved by probing beyond individual cases as they arise?

Coverage might also be improved through better training of journalists. Reporting students should be given rigorous training in judicial organization and procedure, in legal language, in obtaining and understanding legal documents, in using fundamental legal reference materials, in handling the legal problems they themselves may encounter in covering courts and in writing spot news and depth stories about the courts.[9] Such content might be built into reporting, public affairs reporting and depth reporting classes. Outside course work in judicial process, criminology, constitutional law, criminal law and criminal procedure should be strongly encouraged. Attorneys, judges, law professors and others should be brought into the classroom.[10] Nor should the opportunity for such training end with graduation. Reporters might take advantage of short seminars to help them understand the courts;[11] they might ultimately consider appropriate graduate work.[12]

Finally, reporters and editors might more seriously consider complaints that judicial coverage is often inaccurate, one-sided or incomplete, and respond positively to such criticism when it is merited. Reporters may do well to step back occasionally and assess the work they have been doing, the sources they have been using, those sources' motives, and the end result of using those sources. Serious complaints have been leveled at the press from within the trial courts and they must be addressed; introspection can only be useful.

A LOOK AHEAD

I believe the complementary use of three methodologies in this study has added not only richness and authority to the findings but also points clearly to potentially productive future research.

The historical study provided context and background heretofore lacking in our knowledge of newspaper court reporting. It challenged the view that early American newspapers failed to cover local news and warned against the misconception that nineteenth-century court reporting was virtually all sensational. It traced the growing use of diverse news sources and the change in news-gathering techniques.

My approach was essentially anecdotal, taking a fairly broad view of a large time frame. Further historical study might productively be more quantitative, looking, for example, at how frequently various sources appear and what kind of information is attributed to them. Clearly, too, it would seem from my data that such studies focusing on only two or three newspapers over a much shorter time span would be productive and generalizable. Quantitative work such as this should focus on the nineteenth century (and perhaps the twentieth century) since identification of sources is very difficult before 1820.

My observational study is also suggestive. As a case study, it revealed rather dramatically how important some judicial sources are in determining what becomes news, how much chance seems to be involved in what receives press attention, and how very little information actually emerges from the court system. My study was brief. Observation over a period of weeks would seem in order. More important, observation of several court reporters would provide a much stronger base for generalization. Longer observation would also allow for more attention to a reporter's interaction with editors and other reporters, and their role in shaping court coverage. After all, the survey research data from reporters indicated that newspaper policy is a significant factor influencing court coverage, and the reporter I observed was affected by his superiors and seemed to be interested in how his colleagues reacted to his work.

The survey research produced heretofore unavailable descriptive information about the frequency of court reporter-source contact, the types of information for which judicial sources are asked and the types they will provide, the frequency of tips, the ways in which judicial sources use the news media, the frequency of overt reporter-source disagreement, and the nature of sources' complaints about newspaper reporting of courts. Since mine was a study limited to Minnesota state courts, replications in other states would be invaluable. Particularly valuable might be studies allowing comparison among states with different ways of selecting judges. For example, will judges cooperate for different reasons or favor a different press role in states using retention elections than in states with nonpartisan or partisan elections.[13] What about federal judges and U.S. attorneys? Will there be differences between the responses of federal sources and state sources since federal judges are appointed for life and because U.S. attorneys are political appointees?

Finally, it would be valuable to survey and compare sources in trial courts and in other local branches of government, asking identical or similar questions about why they cooperate with reporters, how they use the news media and what they see as the proper role of the press. After all, one of the premises of this study was that reporter-source relationships are different in the judicial branch than in other branches. Such comparison among branches might accomplish directly what this study could do only by inference.

Notes

1. In the eighteenth century, there was no such occupation as reporter, at least as distinguished from "editor."

2. Obviously, my historical research did not include the twentieth century, so this comparison is based on my general observation of trial court reporting.

3. Of course, some protection was also provided under state constitutions; but in 1925, the U.S. Supreme Court first clearly stated, in *dicta*, that freedom of speech and press guaranteed by the First Amendment are among the liberties protected by the due process clause of the Fourteenth Amendment from infringement by the states. The case was Gitlow v. People of State of New York, 268 U.S. 652 (1925). See Zechariah Chafee, Jr., *Free Speech in the United States* (Cambridge: Harvard University Press, 1941), pp. 318–25. Since then, most of the other provisions of the Bill of Rights have also been "incorporated" into the Fourteenth Amendment. See, e.g., Harold W. Chase and Craig R. Ducat, *Constitutional Interpretation*, 2d ed. (St. Paul: West Publishing, 1979), pp. 888–90.

4. Chapter 3 also suggests that attorneys relied on press coverage for advertising purposes.

5. Of course, to the degree that reporters rely on such other cues as the prominence of litigants' names or the unusual nature of the facts as opposed to the broader significance of cases, the odds of legally significant cases being recognized by the press are probably reduced. It may be very difficult for an important case merely of its own weight to attract press attention.

6. The most directly relevant is Donald R. Fretz, *Courts and the News Media* (Reno: National College of the State Judiciary, 1977), although Fretz focuses on fair trial–free press matters. Two other Fretz texts are *Courts and the Community* (Reno: National College of the State Judiciary, 1973) and *Courts and the Public* (Reno: National College of the State Judiciary, 1977).

7. American Bar Association Standing Committee on Association Communications and Division of Communications, *Public Relations Guide for State and Local Bar Associations* (ABA Press, 1979).

8. *Court Guide to Public Information* (St. Paul: Minnesota Supreme Court Information Office, 1979). Public relations officers are becoming somewhat more common in state court systems. See, e.g., Robert A. Martin, "Giving Light to the People: Public Relations for the Courts," *Judicature* 57 (December 1973):190–93.

9. A particularly appropriate text is Lyle Denniston's *The Reporter and the Law* (New York: Hastings House, 1980). Also useful is an American Bar Association Publication, *Law and the Courts* (ABA Press, 1980).

10. For an account of a journalism professor and an attorney team teaching a class in court reporting, see Everette E. Dennis and Michael O. Freeman, "Covering the Courts: A Legal Primer for Reporters," *Quaere*, June 1977, pp. 8–9.

11. Such symposia have been successfully held at the University of Minnesota under sponsorship by press, bench, bar and academe.

12. This is hardly a novel suggestion. See, e.g., "Grant Provides Legal Training for Reporters," *Editor & Publisher*, 9 August 1980, p. 18. See also B. E. Witkin, "A Plan to Send the Media to School," *Los Angeles Daily Journal*, 3 July 1980, p. 4.

13. In a retention election, voters are asked only whether a judge should be retained in office. No competitor appears on the ballot.

APPENDIX A

ROUTINE DAILY COVERAGE, NEW YORK EVENING POST (14 JUNE 1892, p. 2)

NEWS FROM THE COURTS

A QUESTION OF DISCRIMINATION OF FREIGHT RATES

Injunction against the Quebec Steamship Co. and Outerbridge & Co.

Judge Lawrence, sitting at Chambers of the Supreme Court, has recently granted and continued a preliminary injunction against the Quebec Steamship Company and A. E. Outerbridge & Co., its agents, requiring them to transport cargo for G. F. Lough & Co., commission merchants at the Produce Exchange, from New York to Barbadoes by the steamship Trinidad at twenty-five cents per barrel bulk.

From the affidavits on which the motion to continue the injunction was argued, it appeared that until recently the Quebec Steamship Company has enjoyed a monopoly of carrying trade between New York and Barbadoes, and has charged for such transportation at the rate of forty cents per barrel bulk. Within a few months, however, Lough & Co., who are large shippers to Barbadoes, have chartered from time to time the steamship El Callao, which is subsidized by the Venezuelan Government, and so able to take cargo for that voyage, at a profit at the rate of twenty-five cents per barrel. When the El Callao has been in port about to sail for Barbadoes, the Quebec Steamship Company has reduced the rate by its steamship sailing for Barbadoes about the same time as the El Callao to twenty-five cents, which they allege to be about ten cents below the actual cost of transportation.

It has happened several times that Lough & Co., after loading the El Callao, have still had a large amount of cargo for shipment to Barbadoes, and have offered it to the Quebec Steamship Company and tendered freight at the rate charged to other shippers. The Quebec Steamship Company, however, has refused to receive and transport cargo for Lough & Co., except at an increased rate of freight, attempting by discriminating against Lough & Co., to induce them to refrain from chartering the El Callao, and thus to drive that steamship out of the Barbadoes carrying trade, and restore the monopoly which the Quebec Steamship Company formerly enjoyed. For refusing to receive and transport a particular consignment of 1,700 barrels for Lough & Co., except at an increased rate of freight, the injunction was granted.

The counsel for the Quebec Steamship Company attempted to justify this discrimination on the ground that the rate charged to Lough & Co. was barely sufficient to pay the actual cost of transportation. The Court ruled that it was none the less unjust discrimination by a common carrier in violation of its common-law obligation to give equal terms facilities and accommodations to all shippers.

The order continuing the preliminary injunction is apparently the first one ever made by a court of this State against a common carrier for discrimination in freight rates. Henry W. Hardon and Treadwell Cleveland appeared for Lough & Co., and Wilhelmus Mynderse for the Quebec Steamship Company and Outerbridge & Co.

The Sliney Murder Trial—Testimony of The Prisoner

The trial of Michael Sliney for the murder of Robert Lyons was resumed this morning in the Court of Oyer and Terminer, before Judge Ingraham and a jury. The defence put several witnesses on the stand who testified to the defendant's good character. John Corcoran of No. 8 Catharine Street took the stand and testified to the fact that Sliney was in the habit of keeping a dress suit at Lyons's store.

Mrs. Sliney next testified, but the only material point in her testimony was that she went to Lyons's store at 4:30 p.m. on the day of the murder, and saw James Lyons there at 4:30 p.m. Jim has sworn that he did not get to the store until 4:45 p.m.

Mrs. Bridget Brooks, a neighbor of Mrs. Lyons, corroborated her testimony as to this.

Then one of Sliney's lawyers went on the stand, and testified as to the appearance of the store when he visited it the day after the murder.

Sliney, the prisoner, was next called and the first question put to him after he [told] his pedigree was: "Did you strike the blow that killed Bob Lyons?"

"So help me God, I did not," he replied in a low voice and rolling his eyes upwards. He seemed perfectly cool and self-possessed. He admitted writing the note to Father Kean, but said he did so at the request of James Lyons, and he thought the latter was intended for business purposes only. On the Tuesday preceding the murder, which occurred on November 25, 1891, Sliney said he was in the butcher shop, and saw Robert Lyons quarrelling with his mother, and finally throw a steak at her, which hit her in the eye.

He said he had gone there to get $35, which the butcher owed him. Lyons told him to come in next day. Next day was the day of the murder.

Sliney told of his visit on that day to the butcher shop as follows: "I called on him to get the money and my dress suit. It was then between 3:45 and 4:05. Mrs. Lyons and Bob were there. Bob said: 'I can't give you that money until Friday.' 'All right,' said I. 'Will you go and have a drink?' asked Bob. 'I don't mind,' I said, and we went next door and drank mixed ale, and while drinking there, we had a talk about a book. When I returned to the store Bob and I continued to talk and as he talked he leaned with his hands crossed on the handle of the cleaver,

in the butcher shop." Sliney here gave an exhibition to the jurors, handling the fatal cleaver without the least emotion. When Sliney left the butcher shop Mrs. Lyons was there. He returned a few minutes later, and opened the door just in time to see James Lyons running towards the door, with Robert after him, his face all covered with blood. Mrs. Lyons was running after both of them.

"I saw Bob's face clearly," said the witness in a loud voice, "and just as I had caught sight of the two I heard another voice shout, 'Cheese it, Jim, there is Mike Sliney,' and a man jumped into the ice-box. I felt sick and hurriedly slammed the door after me. Later Jim Lyons saw me and begged me not to tell what I had seen, promising to pay me well."

The witness then narrated the occurrences prior to his arrest, and said that when he first went before the Grand Jury he made a statement, telling the truth, and accusing James Lyons of the murder.

"Subsequently you made a confession to Inspector Byrnes accusing yourself of the crime. Why did you do so?"

"Because Jim Lyons told me to do so."

"When did he tell you to do so?"

"On the day he was locked up in the Tombs. I saw him come in a few minutes later, a tier man brought me a note from him in which he said: 'Mike, I understand a man accused of crime cannot claim any property left to him. Now you better clear me and go to Inspector Byrnes and say that you went to see Bob for the $35, and that he refused and kicked and beat you, and that you went out, got drunk, wrote the note to get the boy out of the way, and returned to the store, where Bob beat you again for asking for the $35, and that then you used the cleaver.' That is as near as I can recollect it," said Sliney.

"What did you do with the note?"

"I returned it to the tier man, and agreed to do as Jim asked and did so."

This ended the direct examination and then District-Attorney Nicoll began the cross-examination.

Mr. Nicoll asked: "Why did you obey Jim Lyons as you say you did, and make the confession implicating yourself?"

Here the witness made the only weak point in his answers up to that, when he answered: "He promised me that if I would do so, he would get out and get his share of the money, he would see that I was only convicted of manslaughter, and that when his father died and he got all the money, he would see that I was freed from State's Prison."

"And what was he to give you for doing so?"

"Not a cent."

"Did you not say a while ago that Lyons promised you $5,000?" Judge Ingraham asked.

"Not in the note. The day of the murder he promised me $5,000."

"Why did you consent to sacrifice yourself?" asked Mr. Nicoll.

"I was afraid that if I got out and Jim was sent away, that the people down our way would blame me for opening my trap about the case, and look upon me as a 'sucker.'"

In conclusion he denied that he had ever told Dr. Dana that he had killed "Bob" Lyons.

Dr. Dana by request of the District Attorney, examined Sliney at the Tombs on the 5th instant, so as to be prepared to testify as to Sliney's sanity or insanity, which the lawyers for the prisoner say was very unfair, as they never had any idea of presenting a plea of insanity on their client's behalf.

This ended Sliney's examination and a recess was taken for an hour.

A Lawyer's Alleged Plot To Beat a Client's Creditors Exposed in Court

Judge Bischoff in Common Pleas Chambers, heard this morning queer charges of assault on a lawyer in a public place, of obtaining an affidavit by intimidation and of wife beating, bandied back and forth by counsel engaged in the argument of a motion to continue an injunction in a case odorous with fraud. The action was brought by E. C. Hazard & Co., wholesale grocers, against Cecilia Vera Kieferdorf, Nellie McDonald, and Frederick F. Kieferdorf, to set aside as a fraud upon creditors a bill of sale of the stock and fixtures of his drug store at Columbus Avenue and Seventy-fifth Street, executed in favor of his wife by Kieferdorf on January 22 last; and also a judgment entered against him in February in favor of Nellie McDonald, his wife's sister, in the Court of Common Pleas.

The story of the fraudulent transaction was told this morning in the affidavit of Kieferdorf himself, who, because of conjugal infelicities, has become an ally of the plaintiff in the suit.

During Kieferdorf's absence last winter in Canada, whither he had fled to escape domestic squalls, his wife, according to his statement, forged his name to promissory notes amounting to $7,000 in favor of her sister, Nellie McDonald, a Sixth Avenue hairdresser. No consideration passed for these notes, and they were part of a scheme to avoid the claims of creditors.

The McDonald woman, through Henry M. Honeyman*, a lawyer, started a suit on the note. Heyman then telegraphed Mrs. Kieferdorf, who, under an assumed name, had joined her husband in Montreal to get her husband to instruct Samuel Johnson, an attorney, at No. 270 Broadway, "to take up the case of McDonald against Kieferdorf." The husband did so, using the words quoted. Johnson then made an offer of judgment for $1,070, which was accepted, and judgment was entered against Kieferdorf for that amount.

Kieferdorf came back to this country against his wife's entreaties, and on her representations and those of Heymann that he was in danger of arrest, he kept in hiding six weeks. Presently suit was brought by Hazard & Co., whose claim had been made a subsequent on the stock in the store by the bill of sale, and the fraudulent judgment proceedings concocted by Heymann and the two women, in which an injunction was asked for restraining proceedings under the bill of sale, and the judgment.

To overcome the allegation in the complaint that the promissory notes were forgeries, Heymann took blank notes to Kieferdorf and tried to get him to sign them so that they might be substituted for the forgeries. Kieferdorf wouldn't do it, and then, as the originals bore the stamp of spuriousness on their face, the trio set up the claim that the notes had been destroyed, in order to avoid the presumption against them that would spring from their non production. To support this, Heymann produced in court this morning an affidavit by a Miss Millspaugh to the effect that she saw Kieferdorf tear the notes up.

The counsel for the plaintiff, James J. Allen, charged that Heymann obtained the affidavits by improper means, and asked that the young lady who was present in court be examined privately. Her statement was taken privately, and was to the effect that she was not acquainted with the contents of her affidavit, that when Heymann brought it to her, she refused to sign it, that he then put a pen in her hand and made her sign it without knowing what she was about.

*Also spelled Heyman and Heymann in the original article.

During the skirmishing of counsel, Heymann said that Kieferdorf assaulted him in public, and read a bulletin from Mrs. Kieferdorf to the effect that she had a beating this morning at the hands of her husband. Kieferdorf, outside the court room admitted his hostility to Heymann, says that "he has it in for him yet," and will land him in the penitentiary before he is done with him. Judge Bischoff reserved his decision.

The Case of T. Thomas Fortune

J. Lehman will to-day argue for an appeal in the case of T. Thomas Fortune, colored, editor of the Age, against James Trainor, in the General Term of the Supreme Court, from the decision of Judge Charles J. Truax.

On June 4, 1890, Fortune entered Trainor's saloon at Sixth Avenue and Thirty-third Street, and ordered a glass of beer. The bartender refused to serve him, saying, "We don't serve colored people here." Fortune was finally forcibly put out of the saloon, arrested, and locked up in the Thirtieth Street station. He was discharged in the Police Court the following day. Fortune then brought suit for assault and battery and false imprisonment, and got judgment for $1,016.23.

Court Notes

William E. Nolan of Brooklyn puts in heating apparatus for florists, and put in one for Frank Mankin of that city, which cost about $1,100. Mankin paid all but $300, and this he refused to pay, claiming that the heat from the apparatus was not sufficient, and that in consequence he had lost a crop of 10,000 roses. Nolan sued for the money in the Brooklyn City Court, before Judge Osborne, and the jury gave him a verdict this morning for $200.

Local Court Calendars
(For Wednesday)

Supreme Court General Term before Van Brunt, PJ: O'Brien and Patterson. JJ.—Court opens at 10:30 a.m.; no announcement until 3 p.m.

Supreme Court Chambers, before Beach, J.—Court opens at 10:30 a.m.; motion calendar called at 11 a.m.

Supreme Court Special Term, Part I.—

Adjourned until Monday, June 20.

Supreme Court Special Term, Part II.—Adjourned for the term.

Circuit Court Part I.—Adjourned for the term.

Circuit Court Part II., before Lawrence, J.—Causes to be sent from Part III. for trial.

Circuit Court, Part III., before Truax. J.—Nos. 4234, 765, 3475, 4250, 1654, 1673, 1678, 4246, 313½, 1794½, 1805, 1673, 1699, 1711, 1765, 1767.

Circuit Court, Part IV., before Barrett, J.—Causes to be sent from Part III. for trial.

Superior Court Special Term, before McAdam, J.—Nos. 573, 698, 707, 628, 727.

Superior Court General Term.—Adjourned until Tuesday, July 5, 1892.

Superior Court Trial Term, Parts I, II., and III.—Adjourned for the term.

Surrogate's Court, before Ransom, S.—Case on, No. 773, contested will of Maria E. Hotchkiss at 10:30 a.m.; No. 763, contested will of George B. Taylor at 10:30 a.m.; No. 792, contested will of William H. Post at 10:30 a.m.; Testimony to be taken before the Probate Clerk—Wills of Hannah A. Carman at 10 a.m. Patrick D. O'Halloran, Henry A. Guyan, Lorenz Hauerstein. Patrick Moriarty, Austin D. Thompson, James M. Gilmour, at 10:30 a.m.

Common Pleas Special Term, before Bischoff, jr., J.—Motion.

Common Pleas Equity Term, before Giegerich, J.—Court opens at 11 a.m. No announcement until 4 p.m.

Common Pleas Trial Term, Part I., before Bookstaves, J.—Court opens at 11 p.m. No announcement until 3 p.m.

Common Pleas Trial Term, Part II., before Daly, C. J.—Cases to be sent from Part I. for trial.

Common Pleas Trial Term, Part III., before Pryor, J.—Causes to be sent from Part I. for trial.

City Court Special Term, before Van Wyck, J.—Motions.

City Court Trial Term, Part I., before Newburger, J.—Nos. 1550, 6877, 6357, 6291, 6353, 2595, 6673, 6658, 6756, 6794, 6798, 6844, 5280, 6693, 6862.

City Court Trial Term, Part II., before McCarthy, J.—Nos. 6168, 6083, 6198, 1838, 6236, 6422, 6736, 5138, 6025, 6069, 6815, 6170, 6233, 6084, 6682, 4917, 6148, 4703, 5390, 6824, 6829, 4502, 6326, 6405.

City Court Trial Term Part III., before McGown, J.—Court opens at 10 a.m.

APPENDIX B

TABLE B.1 Percentage of Respondents Working in Counties of Various Sizes

	County Population, Respondents in %								
Respondent Type	Less than 10,000	10,000–19,999	20,000–29,999	30,000–39,999	40,000–49,999	50,000–99,999	100,000 or More	Total*	Number of Cases
Clerks	11%	41	24	6	3	6	9	100%	66
Judges	0	13	16	14	13	3	41	100	63†
County attorneys	9	31	25	6	8	3	19	101	65
Public defenders	0	10	16	13	5	12	44	100	61
Private attorneys	2	5	10	3	3	5	72	100	61
Reporters	17	21	13	4	4	13	29	101	24

* Some totals do not equal 100% due to rounding.

† Number of cases does not include all judges who responded since many serve more than one county. Twenty county judges do so. With the exception of two counties—both in the Minneapolis–St. Paul metropolitan area—all district judges serve more than one county. Thirty-eight percent of 50 district judges responding served districts in this metropolitan area.

TABLE B.2 Percentage of Sources Indicating How Frequently They Appeared in Court During Past Six Months*

	Number of Court Appearances, Answers in %					
Source Type	None	1–10	11–25	More than 25	Total %[†]	Number of Cases
Clerks	11%	12%	21%	56%	100%	66
All attorneys	5	16	13	65	99	191
County attorneys	2	12	11	76	101	66
Public defenders	2	3	8	87	100	63
Private attorneys	13	34	21	32	100	62

* The exact question was, "During the past six months, as best you can recall, about how many times have you been in a courtroom [as a clerk or attorney]? (Note: If you have been in court for more than one case on a day, please count each case as a separate appearance; if one case has taken more than one day, count each day as a separate appearance.)"

[†] Not all totals equal 100% due to rounding.

Selected Bibliography

General Historical Sources

Andrews, Alexander. *The History of British Journalism*. 2 vols. London: Richard Bentley, 1859.

Bleyer, Willard G. *Main Currents in the History of American Journalism*. New York: Houghton Mifflin, 1927.

Brigham, Clarence S. *History and Bibliography of American Newspapers, 1690–1820*. 2 vols. Worcester, Mass.: American Antiquarian Society, 1947.

Chamberlin, Joseph E. *The Boston Transcript*. Boston: Houghton Mifflin, 1930.

Emery, Edwin, and Emery, Michael. *The Press and America*. 4th ed. Englewood Cliffs, N. J.: Prentice-Hall, 1978.

Frank, Joseph. *The Beginnings of the English Newspaper, 1620–1660*. Cambridge: Harvard University Press, 1961.

Gregory, Winifred. *American Newspapers, 1821–1936*. New York: Wilson, 1936.

Hudson, Frederic. *Journalism in the United States*. New York: Haskell House, 1873; reprint ed., 1968.

Hughes, Helen MacGill. *News and the Human Interest Story*. Chicago: University of Chicago Press, 1940.

Kobre, Sidney. *The Development of the Colonial Newspaper*. Pittsburgh: Colonial Press, 1944.

Lee, Alfred M. *The Daily Newspaper in America*. New York: Macmillan, 1937.

Mott, Frank Luther. *American Journalism*. 3d ed. New York: Macmillan, 1962.

Mott, Frank L. *The News in America*. Cambridge: Harvard University Press, 1952.

Parton, James, *The Life of Horace Greeley*. New York: Mason Brothers, 1855.

Payne, George H. *History of Journalism in the United States*. New York: D. Appleton & Co., 1926.

[Pray, Isaac C.] *Memoirs of James Gordon Bennett and His Times*. New York: Stringer & Townsend, 1855; reprint ed., 1970.

Schudson, Michael. *Discovering the News: A Social History of American Newspapers*. New York: Basic Books, 1978.

Seitz, Don C. *The James Gordon Bennetts*. Indianapolis: Bobbs-Merrill, 1928.

Shaaber, Matthias A. "Forerunners of the Newspaper in America." *Journalism Quarterly* 11 (1934):339–47.

―――. *Some Forerunners of the Newspapers in England*. Philadelphia: University of Pennsylvania Press, 1929.

Talese, Gay. *The Kingdom and the Power*. New York: Bantam, 1970.

Thomas, Isaiah. *History of Printing in America*. 2 vols. Worcester, Mass.: Isaiah Thomas, Jr., 1810.

History and Examples of Court Reporting

Baskette, Floyd K. "Reporting the Webster Case, America's Classic Murder." *Journalism Quarterly* 24 (1947):250–57.

Eberhard, Wallace B. "Mr. Bennett Covers a Murder Trial." *Journalism Quarterly* 47 (1970):457–63.

Francke, Warren. "Sensational Roots: The Police Court Heritage." Undated. (Mimeographed.)

[Gill, Thomas]. *Court Reports.* Boston: Otis, Broaders & Co., 1837.

Nordin, Kenneth D. "The Entertaining Press: Sensationalism in Eighteenth-Century Boston Newspapers." *Communication Research* 6 (July 1979):295–320.

Peterson, Ted. "British Crime Pamphleteers: Forgotten Journalists." *Journalism Quarterly* 22 (1945):305–16.

Snyder, Louis L., and Morris, Richard B., eds. *A Treasury of Great Reporting.* New York: Simon & Schuster, 1949.

Wight, J. *Mornings at Bow Street.* London: D. S. Maurice, 1824.

Studies of Judicial Reporting and Reporters

Bereznak, Deborah Unitus. "Public Information Needs Concerning Maryland's Courts—An Assessment." Annapolis, Md., 1979. (Mimeographed.)

Berg, Mary Joan. "Who Are the Newspaper Reporters—And What Do They Think?" *Hennepin Lawyer* 48 (November–December 1978):14–16.

Berger, M. Marvin. "Do the Courts Communicate?" *Judicature* 55 (April 1972):318–23.

Berkson, Larry Charles. *The Supreme Court and Its Publics.* Lexington, Mass.: Lexington Books, 1978.

Center, Harry B. "What Law Should the Reporter Know." *Journalism Bulletin* 4 (March 1927):12–15.

Clayton, James E. "News From the Supreme Court and Justice Department." In *The Press in Washington*, pp. 182–96. Edited by Ray E. Hiebert. New York: Dodd, Mead & Co., 1966.

Community Education Committee of the Young Lawyers Section of the District of Columbia Bar Association. *The News Media and the Washington, D. C., Courts: Some Suggestions for Bridging the Communications Gap.* Washington, D.C.: News Media and Courts Committee of the Young Lawyers Section of the American Bar Association, 1972.

Dennis, Everette E. "Another Look at Press Coverage of the Supreme Court." *Villanova Law Review* 20 (1974–75):765–99.

Drechsel, Robert E. "How Minnesota Newspapers Cover the Trial Courts." *Judicature* 62 (October 1978):195–202.

———, Netteburg, Kermit, and Aborisade, Bisi. "Community Size and Newspaper Reporting of Local Courts." *Journalism Quarterly* 57 (Spring 1980):71–78.

Eimermann, Thomas E., and Simon, Rita James. "Newspaper Coverage of Crimes and Trials: Another Empirical Look at the Free Press—Fair Trial Controversy." *Journalism Quarterly* 47 (1970):142–44.

Ericson, David. "Newspaper Coverage of the Supreme Court: A Case Study." *Journalism Quarterly* 54 (Autumn 1977):605–07.

Goldschlager, Seth A. "The Law and the News Media." Thesis, Yale Law School, 1971.

Grey, David L. "Public Communication of U.S. Appellate Court Decisions." Ph.D. dissertation, University of Minnesota, 1966.

Grey, David L. *The Supreme Court and the News Media*. Evanston: Northwestern University Press, 1968.

Hachten, William A. "Journalism and the Prayer Decision." *Columbia Journalism Review*, Fall 1962, pp. 4–9.

Hale, F. Dennis. "The Court's Perception of the Press." *Judicature* 57 (December 1973):182–89.

————. "How Reporters and Justices View Coverage of a State Appellate Court." *Journalism Quarterly* 52 (Spring 1975):106–10.

Hale, Franklin Dennis. "The Press and a State Appellate Court: News Coverage by Six Dailies of Forty Decisions by the Washington State Supreme Court." M. S. thesis, University of Oregon, 1973.

Johnson, Richard M. *The Dynamics of Compliance*. Evanston, Ill.: Northwestern University Press, 1967.

Lewis, Anthony. "Problems of a Washington Correspondent." *Connecticut Bar Journal* 33 (1959):363–71.

MacKenzie, John P. "The Warren Court and the Press." *Michigan Law Review* 67 (December 1968):303–16.

Monroe, James O., Jr. "Press Coverage of the Courts." *Quill*, March 1973, pp. 20–24.

Newland, Chester A. "Press Coverage of the United States Supreme Court." *Western Political Quarterly* 17 (March 1964):15–36.

Sobel, Lionel S. "News Coverage of the Supreme Court." *American Bar Association Journal* 56 (June 1970):547–50.

Solimine, Michael E. "Newsmagazine Coverage of the Supreme Court." *Journalism Quarterly* 57 (Winter 1980):661–63.

Stanga, John Ellis, Jr. "The Press and the Criminal Defendant: Newsmen and Criminal Justice in Three Wisconsin Cities." Ph.D. dissertation, University of Wisconsin, 1971.

Criticism of Court Reporting

Dennis, Everette E. "How the Press Fails the Supreme Court." *Christian Science Monitor*, 21 February 1979, p. 22.

Forrest, William S. "Trial by Newspapers." *Criminal Law Magazine* 14 (1892):550–58.

Franklin, Marc A. "Reflections on Herbert v. Lando." *Stanford Law Review* 31 (July 1979):1035–58.

Freedman, Max. "Worst Reported Institution." *Nieman Reports* 10 (April 1956): 2.

Gallup, George H., ed. *The Gallup Poll: Public Opinion 1972–1977*. Wilmington, Del.: Scholarly Resources, 1978.

————, ed. *The Gallup Poll: Public Opinion 1978*. Wilmington, Del.: Scholarly Resources, 1979.

Kaufman, Irving R. "Helping the Public Understand and Accept Judicial Decisions." *American Bar Association Journal* 63 (November 1977):1567–69.

Kurland, Philip B. "On Misunderstanding the Supreme Court." *University of Chicago Law School Record* 9 (1960):13.

"Newspaper Reports of Legal Proceedings." *Central Law Journal* 3 (1876):524.

The Public Image of Courts: Highlights of a National Survey of the General Public, Judges, Lawyers and Community Leaders. Williamsburg, Va.: National Center for State Courts, 1978.

Seymour, Whitney North, Jr. *Why Justice Fails.* New York: William Morrow & Co., 1973.

Shaw, David. "Legal Issues: Press Still Falls Short." *Los Angeles Times*, 11 November 1980, p. 1.

———. "Supreme Court Decisions Often Misinterpreted." *Los Angeles Times*, 11 November 1980, p. 3.

———. "Media Coverage of the Courts: Improving but Still Not Adequate." *Judicature* 65 (June–July 1981):18–24.

"Trial by Newspaper." *Albany Law Journal* 11 (1875):248–49.

"Trial by Newspaper." *American Law Review* 18 (1884):1038–40.

Wilmer, Lambert A. *Our Press Gang.* Philadelphia: Lloyd, 1859; reprint ed., 1970.

Influences on Court Reporting

Chafee, Zechariah, Jr. *Free Speech in the United States.* Cambridge: Harvard University Press, 1941.

Chase, Harold W., and Ducat, Craig R. *Constitutional Interpretation.* 2d ed. St. Paul: West Publishing Co., 1979.

Comment. "Contempt by Publication." *Northwestern University Law Review* 60 (1965): 531–49.

Geis, Gilbert. "Preliminary Hearings and the Press." *UCLA Law Review* 8 (1961):397–414.

Gillmor, Donald M., and Barron, Jerome A. *Mass Communication Law.* 2d ed. St. Paul: West, 1974.

Goldfarb, Ronald L. *The Contempt Power.* Garden City; N.Y.: Anchor, 1971.

Graham, Hugh Davis, and Gurr, Ted Robert, eds. *Violence in America: Historical and Comparative Perspectives.* Washington, D.C.: U.S. Government Printing Office, 1969.

Lofton, John. *Justice and the Press.* Boston: Beacon, 1966.

Mueller, Gerhard O. W. "Problems Posed by Publicity to Crime and Criminal Proceedings." *University of Pennsylvania Law Review* 110 (1961):1–26.

Nelles, Walter, and King, Carol Weiss. "Contempt by Publication in the United States." *Columbia Law Review* 28 (1928):401–31, 525–62.

Nelson, Harold. *Libel in News of Congressional Investigating Committees.* Minneapolis: University of Minnesota Press, 1961.

Phillips, Barbara E. "Approaches to Objectivity: Journalistic versus Social Science Perspectives." In *Strategies for Communication Research*, pp. 63–77. Edited by Paul M. Hirsch, Peter V. Miller and F. Gerald Kline. Beverly Hills: Sage Publications, 1977.

Reed, Alfred Z. *Training for the Public Profession of the Law.* Boston: Merrymount, 1921.

Roche, John P. *Shadow and Substance: Essays on the Theory and Structure of Politics.* New York: Macmillan, 1964.

Rothman, David. *The Discovery of the Asylum*. Boston: Little, Brown & Co., 1971.

Sowle, Kathryn Dix. "Defamation and the First Amendment: The Case for a Constitutional Privilege of Fair Report." *New York University Law Review* 54 (June 1979):469–545.

Minnesota Courts

Court Guide to Public Information. St. Paul: Minnesota Supreme Court Information Office, 1979.

Minnesota Continuing Education for State Court Personnel. *Minnesota Clerk of Court Manual*. St. Paul, 1977.

The Minnesota Courts. St. Paul: Minnesota Supreme Court Information Office, 1979.

Judicial Structure

Chester, Alden, ed. *Legal and Judicial History of New York*. New York: National Americana Society, 1911.

Davis, William T. *History of the Judiciary of Massachusetts*. Boston: Boston Book Co., 1900.

Eastman, Frank M. *Courts and Lawyers of Pennsylvania: 1623–1923*. 4 vols. New York: American Historical Society, 1922.

Friedman, Lawrence M. *A History of American Law*. New York: Simon & Schuster, 1973.

Goebel, Julius, Jr., and Naughton, T. Raymond. *Law Enforcement in Colonial New York: A Study in Criminal Procedure*. New York: Commonwealth Fund, 1944.

Kross, Anna M., and Grossman, Harold M. "Magistrate Courts in the City of New York: History and Organization." *Brooklyn Law Review* 7 (1937):133–79.

Pound, Roscoe. *Organization of Courts*. Boston: Little, Brown & Co., 1940.

Washburn, Emory. *Sketches of the Judicial History of Massachusetts (1630–1775)*. Boston: Little & Brown, 1840.

Judicial Selection and Decision Making

Adamany, David, and Dubois, Philip. "Electing State Judges." *Wisconsin Law Review* 1976:731–79.

Berkson, Larry, and Hays, Steven. "The Forgotten Politicians: Court Clerks." *University of Miami Law Review* 30 (Spring 1976):449–516.

Casper, Jonathan D. *The Politics of Civil Liberties*. New York: Harper & Row, 1972.

Cook, Beverly. "Public Opinion and Federal Judicial Policy." *American Journal of Political Science* 21 (August 1977):567–600.

Dubois, Philip L. "The Significance of Voting Cues in State Supreme Court Elections." *Law and Society Review* 13 (Spring 1979):757–79.

Eisenstein, James. *Politics and the Legal Process*. New York: Harper & Row, 1973.

————, and Jacob, Herbert. *Felony Justice: An Organizational Analysis of Criminal Courts.* Boston: Little & Brown, 1977.

Funston, Richard. "The Supreme Court and Critical Elections." *American Political Science Review* 69 (1975):795–811.

Gaziano, Cecilie. "Relationship between Public Opinion and Supreme Court Decisions: Was Mr. Dooley Right?" *Communication Research* 5 (April 1978):131–49.

Goldman, Sheldon. "Judicial Appointments to the United States Courts of Appeals." *Wisconsin Law Review* 1967:186–214.

————, and Jahnige, Thomas P. *The Federal Courts as a Political System.* New York: Harper & Row, 1971.

Grossman, Joel B. *Lawyers and Judges: The ABA and the Politics of Judicial Selection.* New York: John Wiley & Sons, 1965.

Heiberg, Robert A. "Social Backgrounds of the Minnesota Supreme Court Justices: 1858–1968." *Minnesota Law Review* 53 (1969):901–37.

Jacob, Herbert. "Judicial Insulation—Elections, Direct Participation, and Public Attention to the Courts in Wisconsin." *Wisconsin Law Review* 1966:801–19.

————. *Justice in America.* 2d ed. Boston: Little, Brown & Co., 1972.

Jenkins, William, Jr. "Retention Elections: Who Wins When No One Loses?" *Judicature* 61 (August 1977):79–86.

Johnson, Charles A., Shaefer, Roger C., and McKnight, R. Neal. "The Salience of Judicial Candidates and Elections." *Social Science Quarterly* 59 (September 1978):371–78.

Melone, Albert P. "Political Realities and Democratic Ideals: Accession and Competition in a State Judicial System." *North Dakota Law Review* 54 (1977):187–208.

Moos, Malcolm C. "Judicial Elections and Partisan Endorsement of Judicial Candidates in Minnesota." *American Political Science Review* 35 (1941):69–75.

Peltason, Jack W. *Federal Courts in the Political Process.* New York: Random House, 1955.

Richardson, Richard J., and Vines, Kenneth N. *The Politics of Federal Courts: Lower Courts in the United States.* Boston: Little, Brown & Co., 1970.

Rohde, David W., and Spaeth, Harold J. *Supreme Court Decision Making.* San Francisco: W. H. Freeman & Co., 1976.

Ulmer, S. Sidney. "The Supreme Court Opinion as a Communication Device." Paper presented at the annual meeting of the American Political Science Association, Washington, D.C., 28–31 August 1980.

Woodward, Bob, and Armstrong, Scott. *The Brethren.* New York: Simon & Schuster, 1979.

Studies of Nonjudicial Reporting and Reporters

Blanchard, Robert O., ed. *Congress and the News Media.* New York: Hastings House, 1974.

Carter, Roy E., Jr. "The Press and the Public School Superintendent." *Journalism Quarterly* 31 (1954):175–85.

————. "The Press, the Physician, and the Public Health Officer." *American Journal of Public Health* 49 (April 1959):465–72.

Cater, Douglass. *The Fourth Branch of Government.* New York: Vintage, 1959.

Chittick, William O. *State Department, Press, and Pressure Groups: A Role Analysis.* New York: Wiley-Interscience, 1970.

Cohen, Bernard C. *The Press and Foreign Policy.* Princeton, N.J.: Princeton University Press, 1963.

Cox, Harvey, and Morgan, David. *City Politics and the Press: Journalists and the Governing of Merseyside.* London: Cambridge University Press, 1973.

Dennis, Everette E., and McCartney, James. "Science Journalists on Metropolitan Dailies: Methods, Values and Perceptions of Their Work." Paper presented to Symposium on Teaching Science and Environmental Writing, Seattle, Wash., 12 August 1978.

Dunn, Delmer D. *Public Officials and the Press.* Reading, Mass.: Addison-Wesley, 1969.

Dyer, Carolyn Stewart, and Nayman, Oguz B. "Under the Capitol Dome: Relationships Between Legislators and Reporters." *Journalism Quarterly* 54 (Autumn 1977): 443–53.

Fishman, Mark S. "Manufacturing the News: The Social Organization of Media News Production." Ph.D. dissertation, University of California, Santa Barbara, 1977.

Gans, Herbert J. *Deciding What's News.* New York: Pantheon Books, 1979.

Gieber, Walter. "Two Communicators of the News: A Study of the Roles of Sources and Reporters." *Social Forces* 39 (1960): 76–83.

———, and Johnson, Walter. "The City Hall 'Beat': A Study of Reporter and Source Roles." *Journalism Quarterly* 38 (Summer 1961): 289–97.

Hess, Stephen. *The Washington Reporters.* Washington, D.C.: Brookings Institution, 1981.

Hilton, Carol S. "Reporting the Legislature: A Study of Newsmen and Their Sources." M.A. thesis, University of Washington, 1966.

Johnstone, John W. C., Slawski, Edward J., and Bowman, William W. *The News People: A Sociological Portrait of American Journalists and Their Work.* Urbana: University of Illinois Press, 1976.

Lester, Marilyn Jo. "News as a Practical Accomplishment: A Conceptual and Empirical Analysis of Newswork." Ph.D. dissertation, University of California, Santa Barbara, 1974.

Lippmann, Walter. *Public Opinion.* New York: Macmillan, 1922.

Matthews, Donald R. *U.S. Senators and Their World.* Chapel Hill: University of North Carolina Press, 1960.

Molotch, Harvey, and Lester, Marilyn. "News as Purposive Behavior: On the Strategic Use of Routine Events, Accidents, and Scandals." *American Sociological Review* 39 (February 1974): 101–12.

Morgan, David. *The Capitol Press Corps: Newsmen and the Governing of New York State.* Westport, Conn.: Greenwood Press, 1978.

Nimmo, Dan D. *Newsgathering in Washington.* New York: Atherton, 1964.

Rivers, William L. "The Correspondents after 25 Years." *Columbia Journalism Review,* Spring 1962, pp. 4–10.

Robinson, Michael J., and Appel, Kevin R. "Network News Coverage of Congress." *Political Science Quarterly* 94 (Fall 1979): 407–18.

Roshco, Bernard. *Newsmaking.* Chicago: University of Chicago Press, 1975.

Rosten, Leo C. *The Washington Correspondents.* New York: Harcourt, Brace & Co., 1937.

Sigal, Leon V. *Reporters and Officials: The Organization and Politics of News-making.* Lexington, Mass.: D. C. Health & Co., 1973.

Tichenor, Phillip J., Olien, Clarice N., Harrison, Annette, and Donohue, George. "Mass Communication Systems and Communication Accuracy in Science News Reporting." *Journalism Quarterly* 47 (Winter 1970):673–83.

Tuchman, Gaye. *Making News: A Study in the Construction of Reality.* New York: Free Press, 1978.

Tunstall, Jeremy. *Journalists at Work.* London: Constable, 1971.

Judicial-Reporting Skills

American Bar Association Standing Committee on Association Communications and Division of Communications. *Public Relations Guide for State and Local Bar Associations.* ABA Press, 1979.

Dennis, Everette E., and Freeman, Michael O. "Covering the Courts: A Legal Primer For Reporters." *Quaere*, June 1977, pp. 8–9.

Denniston, Lyle W. *The Reporter and the Law.* New York: Hastings House, 1980.

Fretz, Donald R. *Courts and the Community.* Reno: National College of the State Judiciary, 1973.

———. *Courts and the News Media.* Reno: National College of the State Judiciary, 1977.

———. *Courts and the Public.* Reno: National College of the State Judiciary, 1977.

Grey, David L. "Covering the Courts: Problems of Specialization." *Nieman Reports* 26 (March 1972):17–19.

Law and the Courts. ABA Press, 1980.

MacDougall, Curtis D. *Covering the Courts.* New York: Prentice-Hall, 1946.

Martin, Robert A. "Giving Light to the People: Public Relations for the Courts." *Judicature* 57 (December 1973):190–93.

Shuman, Edwin L. *Practical Journalism.* New York: D. Appleton & Co., 1903.

Witkin, B. E. "A Plan to Send the Media to School." *Los Angeles Daily Journal*, 3 July 1980, p. 4.

Methodology

Babbie, Earl R. *The Practice of Social Research.* Belmont, Calif.: Wadsworth, 1975.

Grey, David L. "Interviewing at the Court." *Public Opinion Quarterly* 31 (Summer 1967):285–89.

Heberlein, Thomas A., and Baumgartner, Robert. "Factors Affecting Response Rates to Mailed Questionnaires: A Quantitative Analysis of the Published Literature." *American Sociological Review* 43 (August 1978):447–62.

Lofland, John. *Analyzing Social Settings.* Belmont, Calif.: Wadsworth, 1971.

Phillips, Bernard S. *Social Research: Strategy and Tactics.* 2d ed. New York: Macmillan, 1971.

Riley, Matilda White, and Nelson, Edward E., eds. *Sociological Observation.* New York: Basic Books, 1974.

Rosenberg, Morris. *The Logic of Survey Analysis.* New York: Basic Books, 1968.

Index